Dedication
To Tunde Agbaje-Williams; my link to Anthropology

About the Series

The African Humanities Series is a partnership between the African Humanities Program (AHP) of the American Council of Learned Societies and academic publishers NISC (Pty) Ltd. The Series covers topics in African histories, languages, literatures, philosophies, politics and cultures. Submissions are solicited from Fellows of the AHP, which is administered by the American Council of Learned Societies and financially supported by the Carnegie Corporation of New York.

The purpose of the AHP is to encourage and enable the production of new knowledge by Africans in the five countries designated by the Carnegie Corporation: Ghana, Nigeria, South Africa, Tanzania, and Uganda. AHP fellowships support one year's work free from teaching and other responsibilities to allow the Fellow to complete the project proposed. Eligibility for the fellowship in the five countries is by domicile, not nationality.

Book proposals are submitted to the AHP editorial board which manages the peer review process and selects manuscripts for publication by NISC. In some cases, the AHP board will commission a manuscript mentor to undertake substantive editing and to work with the author on refining the final manuscript.

The African Humanities Series aims to publish works of the highest quality that will foreground the best research being done by emerging scholars in the five Carnegie designated countries. The rigorous selection process before the fellowship award, as well as AHP editorial vetting of manuscripts, assures attention to quality. Books in the series are intended to speak to scholars in Africa as well as in other areas of the world.

The AHP is also committed to providing a copy of each publication in the series to university libraries in Africa.

AHP Editorial Board Members as at November 2018

AHP Series Editors:
Professor Adigun Agbaje, University of Ibadan, Nigeria
Professor Emeritus Fred Hendricks, Rhodes University, South Africa

Consultant:
Professor Emeritus Sandra Barnes, University of Pennsylvania, USA (Anthropology)

Board Members:
1. Professor Akosua Adomako Ampofo, Institute of African Studies, Ghana (Gender Studies & Advocacy) (Vice President, African Studies Association of Africa)
2. Professor Kofi Anyidoho, University of Ghana, Ghana (African Studies & Literature) (Director, Codesria African Humanities Institute Program)
3. Professor Ibrahim Bello-Kano, Bayero University, Nigeria (Dept of English and French Studies)
4. Professor Sati Fwatshak, University of Jos, Nigeria (Dept of History & International Studies)
5. Professor Patricia Hayes, University of the Western Cape, South Africa (African History, Gender Studies and Visuality) (SARChI Chair in Visual History and Theory)
6. Associate Professor Wilfred Lajul, College of Humanities & Social Sciences, Makerere University, Uganda (Dept of Philosophy)
7. Professor Yusufu Lawi, University of Dar-es-Salaam, Tanzania (Dept of History)
8. Professor Bertram Mapunda, University of Dar es Salaam, Tanzania (Dept of Archaeology & Heritage Studies)
9. Professor Innocent Pikirayi, University of Pretoria, South Africa (Chair & Head, Dept of Anthropology & Archaeology)
10. Professor Josephat Rugemalira, University of Dar-es-Salaam, Tanzania (Dept of Foreign Languages & Linguistics)
11. Professor Idayat Bola Udegbe, University of Ibadan, Nigeria (Dept of Psychology)

Published in this series

Dominica Dipio, *Gender terrains in African cinema*, 2014
Ayo Adeduntan, *What the forest told me: Yoruba hunter, culture and narrative performance*, 2014
Sule E. Egya, *Nation, power and dissidence in third-generation Nigerian poetry in English*, 2014
Irikidzayi Manase, *White narratives: The depiction of post-2000 land invasions in Zimbabwe*, 2016
Sylvia Bruinders, *Parading Respectability: The Cultural and Moral Aesthetics of the Christmas Bands Movement in the Western Cape, South Africa*, 2017
Michael Andindilile, *The Anglophone Literary-Linguistic Continuum: English and Indigenous Languages in African Literary Discourse*, 2018
Jeremiah Arowosegbe, *Claude E Ake: the making of an organic intellectual*, 2018
Romanus Aboh, *Language and the Construction of Multiple Identities in the Nigerian Novel*, 2018
Bernard Matolino, *Consensus as Democracy in Africa*, 2018

UNSHARED IDENTITY:
Posthumous paternity in a contemporary Yoruba community

BABAJIDE OLOLAJULO

Published in South Africa on behalf of the African Humanities Program by NISC (Pty) Ltd, PO Box 377, Grahamstown, 6140, South Africa
www.nisc.co.za

First edition, first impression 2018

Publication © African Humanities Program 2018
Text © Babajide Ololajulo 2018

All rights reserved. No part of this publication may be reproduced or transmitted in any form or by any means, electronic or mechanical, including photocopying, recording, or any information storage or retrieval system, without prior permission in writing from the publisher.

ISBN: 978-1-920033-28-6 (print)

Manuscript mentor: Francis Nyamnjoh
Project manager: Peter Lague
Indexer: Michel Cozien
Cover design: Advanced Design Group
Cover photograph: ©Cindy Hopkins / Alamy Stock Photo

The author and the publisher have made every effort to obtain permission for and acknowledge the use of copyright material. Should an inadvertent infringement of copyright have occurred, please contact the publisher and we will rectify omissions or errors in any subsequent reprint or edition.

Contents

Acknowledgements	ix
Foreword	xi
Preface	xiii

CHAPTER 1 Yoruba interconnections, colonial encounters, and epistemological crises — 1

Interconnections in the Yoruba epistemologies	8
The dynamics of 'unequal encounters'	12
Posthumous paternity, levirate and widow inheritance	15
Between identity and identification	18
Organisation of this book	20
Notes	22

CHAPTER 2 The fated grass: Self-representation and identity construction — 25

(Un)veiling the posthumous offspring	26
Being 'born from another man's hands'	28
Ethnographic vignettes: Posthumous offspring and self-presentation	31
Picking up the pieces of a broken self	41
Notes	43

CHAPTER 3 Posthumous offspring and the politics of legitimacy — 47

Borders of legitimacy	48
Legitimacy and the identity of power	53
Posthumous paternity: Where the church stands	59
Notes	61

Chapter 4 Endogenous values, spatial delineation and cultural authenticity — 62

Posthumous paternity and Yoruba cultural authenticity — 64
Levirate or widow inheritance — 69
Revisiting the Yoruba concept of (il)legitimacy — 72
Notes — 74

Chapter 5 Neo-repugnancy: Assisted reproduction as an obscenity — 75

When innovation is negotiated — 79
Children made by doctors — 81
Two faces/phases of the repugnancy doctrine — 84
Help, donation, and making women pregnant — 89
'ART' and the cultural construction of adultery — 92
Notes — 94

Chapter 6 Beyond 'epistemicide': Reclaiming humanity for Africa — 96

Bibliography — 102

Index — 109

Acknowledgements

I owe a debt of gratitude to many individuals and groups for the successful completion of this book. I wish to thank the American Council of Learned Societies (ACLS) and the African Humanities Program (AHP) for the generous grant that enabled me to conduct the research upon which this book is based, and for funding this publication. I am particularly indebted to the Director of International Programmes at ACLS, Andrzje Tymowski, and AHP mentors, Adigun Agbaje, Frederick Hendricks, Bertram Mapunda and Kwesi Yankah for having faith in this work, and for the lively conversations we had at the AHP manuscript development workshop held at the Humura Resort, Kampala, Uganda in June 2015. I also thank my co-participants at the Kampala workshop, Edem Adotey, Pamela Khanakwa, Bernard Matolino, Jacinta Nwaka, Henri Oripeloye, Jean-Baptiste Sourou and Amanda Tumusiime for their insightful comments on my work. My sincere appreciation goes to Barbara van der Merwe of the AHP Secretariat in South Africa for keeping me on my toes throughout the period of preparing the book manuscript.

I am grateful to Francis Nyamnjoh, the development editor AHP appointed to guide the revision of my manuscript, for providing theoretical insights and relevant literature that helped shape the arguments in this book. Indeed, his intervention led to the emergence of an almost new manuscript altogether. I thank my mentors, Tunde Agbaje-Williams, Tunde Lawuyi, Olawale Albert, Omolade Adunbi and Insa Nolte for their support and intellectual guidance. I also owe the programme committee of the Faculty of Arts, University of Ibadan, a debt of gratitude for the seminar that offered me the opportunity to present this work to colleagues and students. In this regard, I thank Adebola Ekanola, Philip Ogundeji, Olatunji Oyesile, Dele Adeyanju and my friends, Akin Odebunmi, Tunde Awosanmi, Doyin Odebowale, Rasheed Olaniyi, Nathaniel Danjibo and Ademola Faleti for their objective reviews and words of encouragements.

Many thanks to senior faculty members and colleagues at the Department of Archaeology and Anthropology, University of Ibadan: Caleb Folorunso, Philip Oyelaran, David Aremu, Samuel Ogundele, Olu Aleru, Raphael Alabi, Aderemi Ajala, Bolanle Tubosun, Segun Opadeji, Francesca Ukpokolo, Kayode Akinsete, Kolawole Adekola and Emuobosa Orijieme. The encouragement and support from them have been immense.

No book would have been written without the contributions of my informants whose privacy I respect by not mentioning them by name. I appreciate you all. My gratitude does, however, go to the traditional ruler of Ilupeju-Ekiti, His Royal Majesty Oba Olaleye Oniyelu, for introducing me to one of my key informants whose input to my overall data was invaluable. I am particularly indebted to Abiodun Ilesanmi, an indigene of the community who lives in Lagos, for allowing me the use of his apartment back home for the entire duration of my fieldwork. To my friends and 'brothers', Otunba Festus Bode Asogbon, Gbenga Edema, Lawson Akintokun, Yomi Oyesaanu, Adeleke Ikuesan, Otito Atikase, Omololu Famose, Adewale Musiliu Busari, Rasaq Adedayo, Habeeb Alli and Kehinde Adejumo, I say a big thank you for the storms we have together weathered. To other wonderful fellows I might have inadvertently overlooked, many thanks too, and kindly accept my apologies for not including your names.

It would not have been possible to complete this work without the inspiration and support from my family. My wife, Lola, and my two sons, Ololade and Folusola are the proverbial cooking tripod that holds the pot. Upon them my scholarship rests. Thank you for the dream we all share.

Foreword

This is a commendable contribution by Babajide Ololajulo. It is a study of significant epistemological relevance to knowledge production informed by the nuanced complexities of being African through relationships of navigation and negotiation of myriad encounters, influences and identity margins. The book highlights, yet again, the important role played by the African Humanities Program since its inception, in grooming and promoting a young generation of African academics and intellectuals at the cutting edge of scholarly debates and innovative research. I have had the privilege of reading and exchanging regularly with Babajide during the development of this book, right from the book proposal stage.

The overall merit of this study is in the rich empirical content on contemporary practices of posthumous paternity and perceptions and lived experiences of and challenges confronting the resultant offspring among the Yoruba caught betwixt and between the attractions of neoliberal notions of individual autonomy on the one hand and resilient collectivism on the other. Central to the study are the tensions and possibilities embedded in identity as the result of individual investment in the process of self-fulfilment in a context where they are compelled to reckon with the collective aspirations and structural forces that define them, sometimes to the point of confining them to the brushstrokes of essentialism and instrumentalisation.

A major contribution of the book is its systematic focus on the epistemological implications or value of the resilience of posthumous paternity despite the overwhelming investment in prevalent market-driven notions of individual autonomy and the cultivation of the self. The study dwells convincingly on the epistemological encounters since colonialism, and the prevalent resistance to zero sum or winner-takes all theorisation of African realities. Among others, the book highlights the following issues to good effect:

i) It foregrounds the extent to which the practice of posthumous paternity is embedded in a Yoruba world and cosmology of interconnections and interdependence;
ii) It discusses how the self-representation of posthumous offspring in the contemporary period easily portrays them as an unfortunate compromise of unequal colonial encounters;
iii) The contested notion of legitimacy based on the contradiction between the cultural logic of posthumous paternity and Western epistemology are

convincingly developed, and equally explored is the idea of a 'sphere of otherness', where dominant Western ideals of being and belonging are 'globalised' or proliferated and 'unorthodoxy' or non-Western (Yoruba and African in this case) are 'pathologised' and 'inferiorised';

iv) The idea of the frontier notion of African communities is broached, by arguing that the resilience of posthumous paternity in a Yoruba speaking community, rather than being perceived and conceptualised as culturally extraneous of the Yoruba, is indeed illustrative of the frontier nature of Ekiti communities and possibly an attestation to the cultural integration and/or flexibility of the Yoruba prior to colonial intrusion and administrative demarcation of bounded cultural geographies;

v) The study shows how asymmetrical power is implicated in the social construction of ethics and morality, with a focus on 'rightness' and 'wrongness'. It does this by exploring and comparing similar ideological premises of Yoruba posthumous paternity and the contemporary practice of assisted reproduction.

I commend Babajide for his orientation on endogenous practices of Africans in general and the Yoruba in particular, and for his remarkable capacity to bring into conversation relevant literature from different disciplines in the humanities and social sciences. Of special mention are his efforts to introduce and inform the study with ideas and perspectives inspired by the often unfortunately dismissed writings of Amos Tutuola, the first Yoruba writer to publish a novel in English that is rich in Yoruba and related cosmologies shared across Africa. The focus on epistemological encounters that are suggested from resilient practices is equally commendable. At a time when the clamour for decolonisation of university education and the call for African epistemologies are very topical in South Africa and across the continent, this book is a worthy and timely contribution.

Professor Francis Nyamnjoh
Head of Anthropology Section
School of African and Gender Studies, Anthropology and Linguistics, University of Cape Town
Rondebosch, July 2018

Preface

In many a Nigerian context, a marriage ceremony in contemporary times is an elaborate performance that occurs in several phases. An elemental aspect is the traditional engagement in which the bride goes through an enthralling ceremony marking her formal separation from her family and incorporation into the groom's family. Although every event is unique in terms of richness of performance, the set of actors involved are similar at all times: bride and groom, bride's parents, groom's parents, paid negotiators, bride and groom's friends, family members and well-wishers. The wedding day, as widely acknowledged, is special to the bride and the groom. Nonetheless, popular understandings of the marriage ceremony also emphasise the importance to parents who presumably see it as the last of their responsibilities to their children.

When, sometime in 2013, a friend, Temmy, invited me to the wedding of one of her kin relations in Ilupeju-Ekiti, a Yoruba-speaking community in the southwest region of Nigeria, it was a traditional Yoruba marriage ceremony enlivened in recent years by exchanges of paid negotiators that I looked forward to witnessing. Apart from fulfilling an obligation to a friend, I also considered the research prospects of the typical lavish reception, the vivacious bridal train, and the *aso-ebi*[1] sensation, all of which have typified most marriage events in contemporary Nigeria.

When I arrived, Temmy revealed some details of the wedding to me. These deviated from the very essentials that I, and I believe most people of my generation, knew about the marriage ceremony among the Yoruba. She spoke about how the bride's paternity was ascribed to her mother's deceased husband who had died many years before the bride was born. Referring to the biological father, she said, 'He will not perform any of the roles commonly associated with the bride's father at marriage ceremonies although he will likely be present at the ceremony.' Those duties that the bride's father would usually perform were, according to her, the exclusive preserve of the bride's 'half-brother', and the eldest son of her mother's deceased husband. The man had travelled from Lagos[2] for that purpose. Temmy told me that the practice of a widow raising children for her deceased husband was an age-long custom in the community. She added that she had also expressed surprise when she first learned of the practice. I had no reason to disbelieve her assertions; more so, since her closeness to the bride's family was never in doubt. As an anthropologist, I considered myself sufficiently knowledgeable about the practice which colonial anthropology termed levirate system, but the reality of this occurring in a contemporary society seemed improbable, and I was indeed anxious to see how the whole marriage event proceeded.[3]

The traditional engagement ceremony took place in the bride's family compound[4] on the very day I arrived. At the well-attended occasion, Temmy surreptitiously showed me a fairly old man seated in the audience whom she described as the bride's biological father. The man, from my estimation, was in his early seventies. He was well dressed for the occasion though not in a particular way that could set him apart from other guests. Interestingly, nothing in his demeanour suggested a filial relationship with the bride. All through the ceremony that lasted for about three hours, the roles of the bride's father were performed by the 'big brother' from Lagos, and an eventful evening was capped when the man performed the symbolic handing-over of the bride to the groom's family. There was no change in actors and their respective roles when the marriage was solemnised at a local council registry the following morning. The man from Lagos, the bride's mother, and one of the bride's siblings were witnesses to the marriage. The bride's biological father graced the event as a passive spectator.

Amidst the usual joy and merriment of a Yoruba marriage ceremony, I tried to conjure up the scenarios that played out in the inner mind of the bride's biological father, and the form of relationship that had over the years existed between him and the bride. I also reflected on the adaptability of the Yoruba traditional value system, both in the past and in a modernised context. As it were, in their proverbs, 'a man is never inconsequential in matters of his possessions' and 'a man's head is not shaved in his absence', the Yoruba seemed to have constructed notions of personal rights, individual entitlements and claim-makings, and active presence. But in the very circumstance I had witnessed, I saw a man humbled by tradition and probably rendered insignificant in a matter of 'his possessions'. Maybe I was wrong.

The marriage ceremony was over, and I returned to Ibadan,[5] but my interest in what I had initially thought a mere unusualness in a Yoruba marriage event was not extinguished. Temmy and I picked up the conversation from where we had stopped in Ilupeju. What could have accounted for the continuity (or should I say resilience) of a practice I had only read about in colonial ethnographic texts? She too had no idea, but wondered why the practice was not in force in other Yoruba communities. To my friend, the idea of ascribing the paternity of subsequent children born by a widow to her deceased husband simply was obsolete and had no place in a 'civilised' society, let alone in a Yoruba community whose populations were Christians in the main. Temmy's reading of the Ilupeju event was not so different from most depictions of endogenous practices that have managed to survive annihilation occasioned by invasion of the African culturescape by Western values and ideals of being human and modern.

The Ilupeju marriage event provokes thought in observers like me about many other endogenous ways of being and meaning-making that are generally believed to have waned and disappeared when the Yoruba and other groups who constitute present-day Nigeria were preyed upon by European colonialism. For instance, even when the Ilupeju ceremony had taken place within a modernised context, the actors enacted various roles ensuing from what is generally alluded to as a traditional cultural value. The most interesting aspect was the element of conformity exhibited by both the physiological father and the bride as well as the fact that the encounter was devoid of tension. In this context, what can be made of the fact that the Yoruba are known to accord such great emphasis to filial responsibility that a physiological father would have fought tooth and nail to have his role as a father acknowledged and restored, if he really had a legitimate claim to make? Why did the bride not weigh in on the stigma of having a 'ghost' as father, particularly since that her physiological father was alive and within reach? But, as witnessed throughout the ceremony, it was a presumably an outdated Yoruba traditional value that was enacted and not all-powerful Western modernity.

The Ilupeju ceremony, in the midst of the proliferation of Western values and a corresponding capitulation of African endogenous epistemologies, no doubt takes on a particular meaning. In addition to inviting introspection on the cultural logics that foster the practice of posthumous paternity, the event speaks to questions of the identity – real or imagined, superior or low-grade, acceptable or objectionable, empirical or superstitious, empowering or disempowering – of a posthumous offspring.[6] Interestingly, these are also key questions raised about African endogenous cultural values. In this context, a surviving posthumous offspring could be thought of as emblematic of a repressed epistemology, enmeshed in an existence and authenticities that are subjects of derision and continuous doubt. In a different way, however, the successful hosting of the marriage event, its unconventionality notwithstanding (I believe many other guests were aware of the posthumous offspring status of the bride), also portrayed a people's indulgence of their own values, even when this does not necessarily equate with acceptance. The ambivalence of posthumous paternity and the connected abstractedness constitute a central issue addressed in this book.

Fieldwork

In the summer of 2014, I received a postdoctoral grant from the American Council of Learned Societies/African Humanities Program (ACLS/AHP) to research a phenomenon I termed posthumous paternity.[7] From July to September 2014, I conducted ethnographic fieldwork in Ilupeju-Ekiti. I returned to the field in July 2015, after attending the AHP manuscript development workshop in Kampala, Uganda.

As a starting point for my research, I successfully circumvented, to a large extent, the problem of language, which is the most common challenge in ethnographic fieldwork. As a native Yoruba speaker, I was able to cope well with the Ekiti dialect, even though I needed to seek help from my field assistant on a few occasions. It was initially something of a surprise that my research mission in the community was known to so many people, even though I had tried to remain as informal and inconspicuous as possible. People easily spotted me as a stranger and the bolder villagers sometimes politely asked me what I was doing in the community. Conversations that ensued from such enquiries led to identification of key informants for the study. I also early on cultivated the habit of frequenting certain places that are well known as locales for gossip and frank talk. These included *ilé emu* (palm-wine drinking spots) and *ìdí ayò*, popular spots where the local *ayò* game and draughts are played. Although I was not much good at either game, I tried to join and successfully used some of the moments to create rapport with other players and as well as to provoke discussions about my research. It is instructive to note that the local *ayò* game and draughts are characterised by informalities and a disregard for seniority and self-restraint among the Yoruba. Hence people that get easily incensed by insults, which are mostly passed under the guise of jokes, are often advised to stay away from *ayò* and draught places. In a way these game centres are informal media par excellence. I learned that the most hidden secret about an individual's identity is often revealed at either *ilé emu* or *ìdí ayò*.

I had, prior to my fieldwork, harboured a notion of my key informants as fairly old people, believing that my hope of gathering rich data depended on them. But as I later realised, older informants were not as helpful as I had envisaged. Quite a number of them were dismissive and the few who showed willingness to speak on the topic of posthumous paternity harped on about the influence of Christianity on traditional Yoruba cultural values, including practices related to widow remarriage and the status of their offspring. On a number of occasions, they gave unsolicited lectures on the Yoruba kinship system and I felt compelled to sit through those interview sessions just to show courtesy. Nonetheless, some sessions occasionally revealed one or two things about the people's culture, some of which became very important to me in the later period of my fieldwork. It took me time to explain the seeming uncooperative attitudes the people in terms of a culture of secrecy, which had underlined the identity of children with 'questionable' paternity and, as well, the continued survival of posthumous paternity. I have provided details of this in Chapter 2. Interestingly, the traditional ruler of the community, rather than speak on the topic, directed me to a man who later proved invaluable as a key informant. The man, acclaimed as the community's public relations officer, was in my estimation in his early sixties, and demonstrated vast knowledge of the community's history.

He knew virtually everybody and was indeed a major factor in the success of my fieldwork.

The interview sessions I had with posthumous offspring were more challenging than I had initially imagined. Apart from the initial problem of informant identification, I was soon confronted with the very problem I was investigating – that of representation. How could I communicate with my informants and yet veil the very reality that many people thought should not be subjected to open discussion? This conundrum invoked a Yoruba proverb: 'No one counts the fingers of a six-fingered man in his presence.' Maybe that was exactly the problem I had – how to engage with posthumous offspring without necessarily subjecting their identity to scrutiny, more so in their presence. Consequently, in conversations, I tried as much as practicable to avoid using the second person singular pronoun and simply adopted the indefinite pronoun, 'one', even when it did not suit my purpose, thinking that this strategy would help to depersonalise the exchanges. My informants, of course, understood I was referring to them and, unlike me, adopted mostly the personalised pronoun 'I' in their own communications. In my mind I approved of the choice of self-reference and felt that at least I would not be perceived as insensitive.

Some notes on the study area

Ilupeju-Ekiti is a Yoruba-speaking community that offers a case study in settlement formation. It was founded from an amalgam of two adjoining ancient communities, Iseta and Egosi. The merger, according to my informants, was initiated in the 1960s by elites of the two communities who, constituted as the Iseta/Egosi Development Association, had constructed a united entity around a series of shared public infrastructure such as a market, post office, maternity centre, secondary school and mosque. The other assumption that drove the union was the notion of political importance and the prospect in leveraging a bigger community to attract development attention from the state. A major challenge to the proposed unification, I learned, was the fate of the traditional authorities of the two communities who were both alive to contemplate the loss of the chieftaincy institutions they had inherited from their forebears. Incidentally, the two rulers died within the space of two years, thereby paving the way for the concretisation of the merger plan. In 1974, a new community, Ilupeju-Ekiti, was created by a government gazette.[8]

Two chieftaincy titles, Apeju and Oba Nla, were subsequently established for the 'newly founded community' – the Apeju as the paramount ruler and the Oba Nla as the second in command or the highest-ranking chief. The two titles are meant to oscillate between the two merging communities. An interesting dimension to the arrangement is the order of succession. It was assumed that upon the demise of the Apeju, the Oba Nla would automatically assume the position of the paramount ruler. The workability of what has so far appeared as a creative chieftaincy deal is yet to be tested as the first Apeju, installed in 1980 was still alive during the fieldwork, although the first Oba Nla passed away in February 2014.

Apart from its political history, Ilupeju-Ekiti is like every other agrarian community that is witnessing fast transformation in its social and economic organisations. The community has a population of about 50 000 inhabitants. This estimate, provided by informants, was not independently confirmed through any official document. Presently, the physical border between the two amalgamated communities is blurred and the population is highly integrated. The community also has a notable presence of other Yoruba dialect groups and non-Yoruba speaking groups, mainly Igbo, who are basically involved in commerce. A highway leading to Abuja, the capital city of Nigeria, runs through the community although I am not sure of the level of influence it asserts on the local economy. Most economic activities, however, including the main market, are formed around the highway.

Epistemological challenges in developing this work

So far, I have outlined the motivation for this work and set out the methods and challenges of data collection. This book is a reflection on the issues of authenticities of African cultural traditions and erosion of endogenous values. However, a rather problematic aspect of this work is its generous referencing of largely Western-based anthropological literature. In itself, this tells the story of an unequal colonial encounter and possibly suggests this work as sufficiently enmeshed in a skewed knowledge-making tradition, which it actually sets out to critique. Nonetheless, what may count for an anomaly and most possibly a contradiction appears to be the very nature of anthropological inquiry in Africa where the bulk of literature on endogenous practices belongs to the category of colonial anthropology. While this literature seems to confirm the centrality of Western scholarship to the construction of African worldviews, its texts compel not just a revisit to or reinvention of colonial narratives (an objective of this book), but also speaks to the marginal positions of Africans in the entire processes of producing knowledge about their continent.

On the surface, it appears illogical to foreground in Western scholarship (Foucault, Goffmann, Sokerfeld and so on) a book that seeks to make a case for endogenous African epistemologies. But then, the pertinent question is whether one can validly define contemporary Africa outside of the historical processes that have come to shape current realities on the continent. Here I consider the experiences of incorporation (particularly in the sense of enthronement of the neoliberal individual) not just as transforming but equally a core aspect of African realities. Interestingly, notion of the bounded and independent self, communicated in the works of many Western theorists of self and identity, often contrasts the African idea of the self as social and defined basically in terms of 'we-existence' or man-in-relation-to-others (Okolo 1992). For instance, a unique aspect of African philosophy (Placide Tempels, John Mbiti, Julius Nyerere, Tom Mboya) is its creation of a universe of interdependence, which by its form and functionality recognise the incompleteness of man, thereby establishing the self as existing within a complex web of social relationships encompassing both the living and the 'living-dead'. Most often formulated in terms of communal supremacy, this worldview, shared across many African societies, while promoting the idea of 'a being-in-community', is shown to diminish or perhaps undermine the autonomy of the individual, typically representing an inability to seek or pursue goals independent of the community. Scholars have alluded to this as the 'self-problem' in African epistemologies (Okolo 1992). Although individual agency in many traditional African societies is rarely in doubt, being a core social determinant and evidence of the spiritual character of man, little or no evidence exists to show that it constitutes a problem or conflicts with the more popular idea of a social self. In effect, the sense of individuation, which underlies various responses of posthumous offspring[9] and as well corresponds to different ways of being, cannot be separated from a modern social order. Foucault's approach to modernity envisions it as an attitude, and particularly one that questions and transfigures the present (1997, 309). Here, he may be seen to be sympathetic to the colonial enterprise and its disruptive agenda. But his logic, basically criticism of the history of modernity, also challenges every form of status quo and is supportive of transgression, thereby posing in equal term a challenge to Western modernity, particularly in the realm of the subjugating techniques of coloniality – a structure of power Mignolo (2011) once described as 'the darker side of Western modernity'. In other words, there is in Foucault, an ambivalence toward norms – moving against tradition on the one hand while, on the other hand, seeking freedom from subjugation.

Can it then be said that the stance of Western scholarship on colonial encounters with African societies was neutral in a way that makes it possible to delink this scholarship from the colonial mould of power as well as postcolonial knowledge production about Africa? Realities show that this can hardly be the case. After all, we are not unmindful of anthropologists' participation in the colonisation of Africa, and particularly their resort to binary opposites to establish the superiority of European civilisation. It does not matter much whether this class of anthropologists is described as armchair in so far as their ethnographic accounts form the basis of interpreting and representing the African continent and its peoples. It is in this vein that European writing about Africa as MacGaffey (1981, 265) submits, 'presents itself in Africa with uniform authority as the product of sciences', and many times prescribing the Westernising path as the one and only route to achieving industrial production and market economy. And then there are the Western scholars who provided the framework for imperial governance and constituted themselves into advisers of sort. In respect of the scale of services they could offer the colonial administrator, Bronislaw Malinowski wrote:

The practical man should be asked to state his needs as regards knowledge on savage law, economics, customs, and institutions; he would then stimulate the scientific anthropologist to a most fruitful line of research and thus receive information without which he often gropes in the dark. (Malinowski 1929, 22)

The expert knowledge on Africa, which colonial anthropologists like Malinowski make claim to, is nothing more than ethnocentric prejudices that contrast with the ideals of Western modernity. The idealistic perspectives of colonial anthropologists have, in a way, assisted colonial administrators to gain deeper insights into indigenous culture and as well dominate it (Mudimbe 1988).

Western scholarship engagement with the colonial order is also obvious at the level of the politics of knowledge production about Africa. Though most colonies achieved independence in the 1960s, knowledge production has remained a contested terrain where Western scholars, some of whom prefer an Africanist identity, and their African counterparts compete for authenticity and authority. Ordinarily, a dichotomy between foreign and local will appear superfluous considering the notion of universality inherent in modernity. But then, charges of misrepresentation or misinterpretation of African worldviews levelled against Western scholars by Africans are so rife as to warrant calls for a decolonised scholarship. Moreover, the surge in intellectual nationalism in Africa's post-independence era draws attention to the readiness of Africans to write their own stories. Interestingly, the engagements of the two competing scholarships (Africanists and Africans) have been largely unequal, following in the tradition of the encounter between the colonisers and the colonised. A colleague of mine once jokingly suggested that Western scholars are sceptical of the quality of intellectual production many African scholars are capable of and, as such, would not leave Africa to the Africans. Such a view, abrasive in its jocularity and perhaps excessively generalised, is indicative of a discontent with Western scholars' intellectual hegemony. But it is not only about Western scholars being unconvinced; there is much evidence to suggest that many citadels of learning in Africa are desirous of endorsements of their scholarships from the West as a sign of authenticity. With policies such as those which require African academics to be published widely in foreign (Western) journals as a condition for promotion, the fetishism made of Western awards and fellowships, and an assessment process that only gets completed after the Western seal is affixed, Africans themselves seem to unwittingly yield to an inglorious dependency narrative.

Concepts like African epistemology and Western modernity, well employed in this book, are laden with multiple interpretations and, as such, cannot be simplified in a way that would flatten their meanings. For instance, inherent in the idea of Western modernity, as a regional configuration, is the assumption of multiple modernities or even the suggestion of modernity in continuum, a vivid case of modernity at large, to echo the title of Arjun Appadurai's (1996) book. Apart from capturing the cultural elements associated with the European inspired Age of Enlightenment, by Western modernity I mean the apparatuses of colonial subjectivity, including material and institutional complexes that brought about large-scale cultural transformation in the colonies. Thus, beyond it being a category of events and a particular social order in history, Western modernity carries an ideological cross of producing colonised subjects in the image of European modes of being. Put another way, it entails the most critical elements of Christian ethics as well as European etiquettes, which often pass as civilization. My thought on the change instigated in African worldviews by Western modernity is, therefore, essentially incorporative, as I tend to argue all through this book. In other words, the idea of Western modernity I advance takes in the aspect of colonial power and missionary projects, all of which have and continue to engender far-reaching alterations in African societies.

Regarding a conception of Africa, I have in this work the challenge of essentialising the continent, and disregarding tendencies that point toward plurality. Although there has been a long-standing debate about representation of the continent – exemplified in the works of Ayittey, Kagame, Hountondji and others – my attitude in this work is not to deny a domain of knowledge that is particularly African, much the same way a Western episteme has never been in doubt. In other words, while taking due cognisance of propositions about an African reality, by which it is meant a uniform notion of being or a standardised worldview on existence, I give recognition to such cultural distinctiveness across African societies that suggests multiple realities even amidst the homogenising effects of colonial experience. This orientation has a particular effect. For one, it means there is nothing like African culture or an African way of life, and that every hypothesis on cultural unity is a ruse. Nevertheless, my aim is not to be entirely dismissive of a collective consciousness for Africans or repudiate their historical connectedness, at least for the sake of a necessary nationalism. But it is my hope that this book will contribute to existing commentaries on the humanity of Africa and the resilience of the continent's endogenous epistemologies.

Notes

1   In Nigeria, *aso-ebi* refers to the uniform dress or commemorative attire which family

members and sometimes friends and well-wishers wear during special occasions such as wedding ceremonies and funerals.

2. Lagos is the commercial nerve centre of Nigeria and the former capital of the country.

3. Chapter 1 contains a comprehensive discussion of the levirate system.

4. The Yoruba traditional marriage is referred to as engagement ceremony in contemporary Nigeria.

5. Ibadan is a city in southwest Nigeria

6. Posthumous offspring as applied in this book are children born by a widow but have their paternity ascribed to the deceased husbands of their mothers rather than to their biological fathers. The Ilupeju posthumous offspring refer to children a widow bears while she lives in her deceased husband's house. They are regarded as legitimate children of their mother's deceased husband and are socialised to see themselves as such. They bear no social or economic relationship with their biological father whom they may acknowledge only to the extent of his affinity with their mother. They also regard the older children the posthumous father sired in his lifetime as siblings who are committed to them for socialisation and for support.

7. Posthumous paternity is the idea of ascribing the paternity of subsequent children born by a widow to her deceased husband.

8. I did not really understand the idea of creating a new community by government gazette, although the term 'gazette' refers to the official publications of government containing major decisions needed to be communicated to the public.

9. It should be noted that due to the sensitive nature of the subject of this work, my informants are denoted by pseudonyms, except in instances where I do not consider the data sufficiently sensitive.

1

Yoruba interconnections, colonial encounters, and epistemological crises

The Nigerian play, *The Gods are not to Blame*,[1] was a ready menu for students of literature in English during my days at secondary school. Like many African literary works, it was laced with proverbs. A particular one, 'A butterfly thinks itself a bird' was very popular and as students we had employed it loosely to describe classmates thought wannabes. Of course, the full import of the proverb was actually known to be beyond someone being a pretender, but no one dared question the other person's identity openly. However, there were a few occasions when classmates engaged in fights over name-calling, especially where paternity had been the subject of derisive jokes. In 'A butterfly thinks itself a bird' is a notion of identity as bounded, a case of either you are or you are not. But, also implicit in the proverb is the prospect for identity renegotiation or redefinition, even where such seems improbable. Hence, identity – voluntarily acquired or imposed – may instil in individuals or a group, varying consciousness of empowerment or disempowerment, inclusion or exclusion, rights and privileges and other forms of awareness bordering on space and relationality. It was a constellation of the identity construct that filled my mind when I arrived at Ilupeju to conduct research into posthumous paternity, and possibly look for butterflies that could indeed be birds.

One of the numerous arguments often advanced against European colonialism pertains to the marginality of Africa and her cultural traditions (Rodney 1972; Amin 1972). In Nigeria, for instance, posthumous paternity was a functional custom of some groups up till the time customary laws were developed as part of the statutes for colonies. Then, the British colonial authority declared posthumous paternity, among other African family system and procreation practices such as woman-to-woman marriage and 'ghost' marriage, 'repugnant to natural justice, equity and good conscience'.[2] The suppression, no doubt, fitted into a British-inspired process of social transformation that had already seen the political organisation and belief systems of Africans in various societies subdued. With the codification of customary laws, the colonial authority also became the sole source and confirmer of morality, even as Western values inevitably assumed the standard of good conduct for Africans. Many of the elites, in those early days, were instantaneously drawn into the lifeworld of Western assimilation, which then wore the garb of civilisation and perhaps still does. As missionaries, administrators and politicians, African elites helped propagate the ideology of Western cultural transcendence by quickly adopting what was then regarded as 'a new way of life'. A few, however, showed disaffection, not just with the Westernising logic, but with a system that rendered African worldviews inferior and uncanny. Such cynicism manifested well in the works of some first-generation African fiction writers and in instances of deliberate contravention of colonial laws.

Writing about the exquisiteness of their cultures has been an established way by which Africans protest Western cultural imperialism. However, any recent encounter with a supposed cultural fossil would seem by far adequate to recount the story of resilience and of rootedness of African values. The evidence of posthumous paternity in Ilupeju which I found when I attended a marriage ceremony in the community is more than a simple triumph of an endogenous value[3] or an affirmation of cultural resilience. Beyond that, the reality occurs as contestation of a unidirectional reading of modernity, as 'a general break with all sorts of pasts' (Appadurai 1996, 3), and a reflection of the interconnections inherent in a Yoruba modernity that is mostly negotiated and internally driven.

In this book, I attempt to employ the identity of posthumous offspring as a prism for interrogating the complex issues of recognition, representation and power relations thrown up by the fact of colonial powers deflating African values, a condition Francis Nyamnjoh aptly refers to as 'epistemicide' (2012, 129). I argue that posthumous paternity, rather than being an uncomplicated creative kinship practice aimed at lineage perpetuation as suggested in the extant literature (Radclife-Brown 1950; Gray 1964; Abrahams 1976), is indeed a product of a worldview woven around the multiple interconnections and interdependences that often characterise family systems, community and intergroup relations in pre- and postcolonial African societies. This book depicts African ideas of 'being and becoming' not in the zero-sum logic of linear progression, but within the recognition of entanglements and continuities that provide for the future in the past and the past in the future (or the dead in the living and the living in the dead, the natural in the supernatural and vice versa). This ideology reflects well in the everydayness of the Yoruba and is symbolised in the naming system and humanisation of the supernatural. However, the encounter between Yoruba epistemology and Western cultural values, as I will argue, occasions a suppression, but not extinction, of the endogenous culture and engenders in it a kind of adaptability. Meanwhile, the power dynamics between Western modernity and a practice such as posthumous paternity tend to deprive the latter of humanity and in effect produces posthumous offspring as an unusual identity.[4] In their reactions, posthumous offspring, I argue, configure self in terms of individual life experiences, adopting more or less individual stances, which Foucault (1988) has described as technologies of the self, thereby producing a notion of their identity as unshared.

Specifically, the interest of this work lies in understanding how posthumous offspring embodied the contradictions in Africanness and Western modernity. It seeks to offer insight into the implications of individuals becoming the vessels of conflictive cultures, and the adaptive mechanisms that are employed for social integration. I ask a number of questions bordering on the social positions of posthumous offspring within the lineage system. For instance, among other questions, I ask how posthumous offspring make sense of and manage their identity within the extended family; whether they feel a strong sense of belonging in the extended family system; how they construct self and relatives, what happens when their interest in a patrimony conflicts with that of another member of the patrilineage; whether the circumstance of being a posthumous offspring inhibits personal aspiration and drive for honours; and how the idea of a connection outside blood relatedness shapes or reshapes both the basic ideology of belonging and the social advantage attached to kinship. These constitute questions of socialisation and rights. But beyond that they reflect the unresolved conflicts created in the African mind as a result of the colonial encounter. Here, the work assumes that the emphasis placed on blood ties in Yoruba society and the role of social identity in assessing patronage would hinder the participation of posthumous offspring in public spaces, especially in arenas where resources are contested. The possibility of them thinking of their personalities in abridged terms, the work suggests, can hinder their self-actualisation. Thus, even when posthumous paternity would simply stand for continuity of a cultural tradition, the juristic status of offspring in a contemporary Yoruba society needs to be explained, especially amidst the role of genetic links as a strong factor for inheritance.

As an ethnographic study of an endogenous practice, this book illustrates how the reality of posthumous paternity and offspring in a contemporary society attests to the virility and enduring nature of Yoruba cultural tradition. The instance of posthumous offspring in a 21st-century Nigerian community unarguably shows that kinship practices are not all that susceptible to extraneous agencies of cultural change. For instance, it is instructive that practices such as witchcraft, which is very much about relations of intimacy and their management, are much alive, as attested to by the proliferation of witchcraft themes in Nigerian (Nollywood) movies, writings and church engagements. The failure of legalistic pronouncements to obliterate what Ebeku (1994, 54) describes as 'a custom which attributes "fictitious genealogy" to a child' demonstrates resilience on the part of a people's cultural tradition. From every indication, continuity implies a level of commitment to preserving an age-long tradition, and validating a local custom outside jurisprudential encumbrance. But there is also no doubting the kind of transformation that has been witnessed within both the structural and institutional frameworks from which legitimacy is supposedly derived. This is indicative of a commitment on the part of present-day Yoruba people to ensuring continuity of traditions while simultaneously embracing change, thereby bringing tradition into conversation with local and exogenously induced ideas of modernity. Put differently, the Yoruba people of Nigeria are actively determined to embrace modernity and tradition simultaneously as dynamic realities. Such ambivalence or refusal to yield to the diktats of zero-sum games of winner takes all (Nyamnjoh 2015), we are compelled to argue, promotes secrecy and hypocrisy among the people and situates the practice of posthumous paternity within the marginal position it occupies in the local construction of kinship. It is in this particular regard I explore the aspect of cultural continuity, which apparently the practice connotes, while situating my analysis within the frame of sociocultural dynamics of a conflictive identity.

This book also explores the similar ideological premises of Yoruba posthumous paternity and assisted reproduction technology (ART). With the gradual localisation of ART in Nigeria and its use on a global scale, it might become easier to see asymmetrical power being implicated in the social construction of rightness and wrongness. The questions of offspring legitimacy, inheritance and rights to succession, which colonial anthropology has asked in regard to the practice of a widow raising children for her deceased husband, equally underlie the earliest debates on assisted reproduction technology practices. Shore (1992, 295), for instance, has seen the challenges posed by new reproductive technologies as pertaining to 'ideas about motherhood, paternity, biological inheritance, the integrity of the family, and the "naturalness" of birth itself'. Similarly, other scholars like Laing (2006) and Simpson (2001) have argued that artificial reproduction does not just have implications for personhood, identity, ancestry, fraud and perjury, family and property law, inheritance and intestacy, but also for the people conceived by these means. In like manner, Bob Simpson posits that posthumous conception as *in vitro* fertilisation 'loosens the "natural" grounds upon which normative constructions of marriage, paternity, and mortality are built' (2001, 2). I also found out quite early during my fieldwork that genitors of posthumous offspring and other children of questionable identity in Ilupeju were considered as 'helpers'. I am particularly interested in how this image compares with what Simpson (2013) regards as the questions of relationality and exchange in ART. These and many more questions about the Western ideal of assisted reproduction readily bring to mind a Yoruba proverb that probes what the difference is between the craniums of a monkey and a gorilla, basically as a way of denouncing instances of double standards of morality. In the examples of Yoruba posthumous paternity and assisted reproductive technology, we seem to be confronted with a case of similar phenomena being accorded dissimilar rationalisations. A central argument contained in this book, therefore, is that unusualness, especially as it pertains to endogenous African values, is produced from a rationalising epistemology whose ascendancy to the level of magisterial universalism can be explained only in terms of Western roots.

Meanwhile, the aspect of power, which includes the material and psychological advantages available to people within public space, is also of immense importance in a neoliberal environment where people are not only engaged in unmediated struggles over scarce resources but have also employed all sorts of unconventional strategies to further personal goals. It is definitely in relation to power that the struggle for personhood finds in identity an exclusionary device for mitigating social and economic competitions. Thus, a core aspect of this work is about identity as a cultural construct and its interface with power, as well as the power of identity and culture. Within the context of power and its tendency for disempowerment, the authenticity of endogenous values is questioned, while it is shown how posthumous offspring find their legitimacy subjected to the contemporaneous norms that are, of course, extraneous to the culture that validates their existence. This is an argument I pursue in Chapter 3 of this work.

Anthropologists from Africa and the West have documented the practice of a widow bearing children in the name of her deceased husband in several African societies. Notable examples are the Nuer of South Sudan (Evans-Pritchard 1951), the Zulu of South Africa (Gluckman 1950), the Tswana of Botswana (Schapera 1950), the Nandi and Luo of Kenya (Oboler 1986; Potash 1986) and the Igbo of southeast Nigeria (Okonjo 1992; Korieh 1996). Strangely, none of the early notable ethnographic works on the Yoruba has alluded to posthumous paternity as a kinship practice of the people. Earliest mentions of it in the literature on traditional cultural practices in Nigeria associated posthumous paternity mostly with the Igbo. Offering a nuanced explanation for the proliferation of analogous cultural values across ethno-regional spaces requires the denunciation of the artificial borders erected by colonialists to separate communities on the basis of distinctive languages, which, unfortunately, were considered strong markers of cultural differences. In essence, I argue that survival of cultural traits is likely to be consequent upon multiplicities of bases rather than a restricted space with which a cultural trait is associated. Thus, rather than thinking of endogenous cultural traits as bounded and existing in isolation, I propose an idea of crossroads or an intersection of values driven by commonality of experiences. The crossroads, I suggest, produce possibilities that manifest in relatedness and sometimes in contradictions. The instance of posthumous paternity in Ilupeju, I therefore argue, challenges existing ethno-regional delineation of the culture of posthumous conception, which associates the practice with a limited section of Nigeria, and suggests a similarity of values across various African societies beyond that which is generally acknowledged in the extant literature.

Two major approaches are discernible in existing explanations on the practice of a widow bearing children in the name of her deceased husband. The first one defines the practice in terms of necessity for lineage perpetuation, and the other is hinged on the socio-economy of bridewealth (Evan-Pritchard 1945; Kirwen 1979). In both, the agency of the dead seems to be inverted and continuity of life is made a prerogative of the living. However, in many African epistemologies, the dead do not exist completely outside of the world of the living, but are expected to utilise their ethereal nature for continuous participation in human everydayness (Mbiti 1969). Among the Yoruba, for instance, the dead are associated with a wide range of bodily manifestations and possibilities: power, transmutations and limitlessness, among others. This book foregrounds posthumous paternity in the range of potency and potentialities commonly associated with the dead by the Yoruba. In this connection, if Amos Tutuola's works are not simply to be dismissed as literary fantasies, but as grounded in Yoruba culture and cosmology, we can then see them as excellent examples of thick descriptions (in Geertz-like fashion) of these associations between the dead and the living, the visible and the invisible, the virtual and the real (Nyamnjoh 2012, 2015).

Apart from posthumous paternity, another paternity custom reported in Ilupeju seems relevant to the arguments made in this book. My informants spoke of a practice in which a woman (in a subsisting marriage) may bear a child or children 'from the hands of another man'. This example was more common in cases of adultery. The general opinion people had of the genitor was of a 'helper' who had no paternity claim whatsoever on the offspring. This practice, I argue, also attests to the embeddedness of paternity. However, beyond the paternity locus that runs through posthumous offspring and children born 'from the hands' of men other than the mothers' husbands, there is the element of matriarchal power implanted in the notion of paternity. Taking paternity from a genitor is, for all intents and purposes, indicative of what I term biological irrelevancy in the local construction of conception. This book provides an explanation for this in the second chapter. This view is also about understanding that paternity is socially constructed and not merely a biological function, which seems to be the prevalent idea in the West where Margaret Thatcher once famously declared that there is no such thing as society. It is also a way of questioning the very narrowly materialistic or economic basis of relationships, by bringing into the equation and in many regards prioritising the moral basis of relationships – of the Ubuntu type – that a person is a person because of others, and success is meaningful only to the extent that it is inclusive.

From the aforesaid, two theoretical positions are implicated in this study. First is cultural resilience as an analytical standpoint that suggests triumph over adversity, and hopes for a future that is framed with endogenous ideals as a major part of the equation. As Mugambi (2002, 116) observes, 'World-views tend to be so resilient that they will re-emerge after many centuries of suppression.' Resilience constitutes a veritable instrument for introspection, and in it I found a way of arousing the African intellectual mind on the inanity of wholly submitting to a stereotypical ascription of the continent's endogenous epistemologies. In other words, I have considered the power of self-(re)definition strong enough to stimulate positive orientation in every attempt to (re)claim humanity for Africa. Thus, explaining the contemporary identity of the posthumous offspring and perhaps the exoticness in a neoliberal context will require understanding the Western epistemological order by which endogenous cultural values are inferiorised, while equally considering its effects, not in terms of permanence or irreversibility, but mainly in engendering dual and conflicting consciousness in the minds and behaviours of Africans.

The second theoretical perspective dwells on anthropological treatment of self and identity. Here, the objective is not to treat posthumous offspring as an organised assemblage of individuals with well-articulated and shared interest. Although they constitute a social category by virtue of otherness, their notion of themselves and relations, as I would argue, is not based on a sense of collective identity but rather on individual subjective experience of the self. Each posthumous offspring, from what I have observed, represents his or her individual identity differently and in accordance with the values imbibed during socialisation. Here I draw largely on Foucault's 'Technologies of the self' and Bourdieu's (1984) idea of *habitus* to explicate the strategies employed by posthumous offspring to negotiate membership and participation in a milieu dominated by an epistemology that contradicts that which confers on them authenticity. I align well with Martin Sökefeld's conclusion on the subject of self and identity when he said that 'it is impossible to conceive of the actions of individuals embracing a plurality of identities without referring to the self' (1999, 418). However, such submission does not suggest an orientation toward a psychological treatment of identity as individualism. Instead, it is a line of thought that largely flows from Anthony Cohen's (1994) consideration of the self in anthropology as aimed towards problematising the relationship between the individual and the social (cited in Sökefeld 1999, 419). In other words, in the absence of a sense of 'we', posthumous offspring are expected to navigate the bounds of their identities more or less as individuals, while employing different elements of the 'technologies of the self' to enforce participation in the social milieu. Nonetheless, they may sometimes have to engage in self-denial and active self-restraint (Weber 2005[1930]) in order to have a sense of being and belonging.

This study thus focuses on the social representation of posthumous offspring with particular attention paid to their subjective experiences. Though it might lack the holistic explorative characteristics of ethnography, it is nonetheless offered as an interpretation of a cultural fossil. It is an attempt to employ ethnographic data to historicise a process of epistemological reversal, which Nyamnjoh (2012) describes as devaluation of Africans and glorification of Europeans. Through qualitative methods of interviews and life histories I explore the lifeworld of posthumous offspring, the experience of their exotic identity, which correlates with identity crises, and the encumbrances occasioned by what Goffman (1969) considers as identity pathologisation.

Interconnections in the Yoruba epistemologies

An aspect of African cultures which has received wide attention from scholars is the sense of community that is dominant in social relationships. For one, identity among Africans is not etched on the individual but expressed in terms of membership of a kin group, lineage and wider social groupings such as the clan simultaneously (Llyod 1955). This sense of community also reflects in the idea people have of the relationships they bear not just with members of the extended family network but also with their dead relations. Ideas about ancestors vary across Africa but every instance suggests unbroken ties between kin relations even after the separation occasioned by death. Moreover, the responsibility demonstrated toward dead relations through burial and transformational rituals performed on corpses (Hertz 1960; Mbiti 1969; Turner 1969; Palgi and Abramovitch 1984; Bloch 1988; Davies 2000; Wagner 2013; Lawuyi 2015) are all linked to the idea of the dead and the living as bound together in a relationship in which individual forms and functions are in a perpetual state of flux. Generally, African realities are marked by relational contemplations and deep philosophical thoughts that are demonstrated in myths, proverbs and numerous other ideological and material expressions. These constituted the framework of a system that unarguably functioned very well until colonial intrusion, which validly or otherwise has since remained a subject of scholarly debates.

In Yoruba cosmology, life is not subject to obliteration, as there often remains a vestige of it, either perpetuating it or symbolically connecting it to another life. The Yoruba belief about their universe stresses *aye* (earth) and *orun* (heaven) not as bounded spaces but rather as a continuum (Mbiti 1969; Abimbola 2006). Specifically, the Yoruba creation myth about a gold chain, which hung from the sky down to the earth, and of deities who criss-cross heaven and earth, speaks to a spatial interconnection and to the crafting of the Yoruba universe as a pluralistic assemblage. 'Being and becoming' (Nyamnjoh 2015, 9) in the Yoruba epistemology, therefore, are landscapes of possibilities, devoid of spatial limitation and entrenched in an ideology of transformational freedom. For instance, although the soul of an aged dead who has fulfilled *ayanmo* (destiny) is said to go to *orun* where it joins the league of ancestors (Taye 2013), such a soul is not confined but rather operates within the possibilities allowed by the interactional flows that occur between the here and the hereafter. A similar belief among the Igbo of southeast Nigeria is expressed by Chinua Achebe in the following lines:

> The land of the living was not far removed from the domain of the ancestors. There was coming and going between them, especially at festivals and also when an old man died, because an old man was very close to the ancestors. (Achebe 1958, 97)

With the kind of flexibilities inherent in spatial relationality, the idea of death leading to total removal from the lineage is far-flung. The Yoruba, in theorising the continuity of life, proverbially construct a transformational relationship between fire and ashes on the one hand and banana tree and the suckers on the other hand.[5] Thus, they regard continuity as existing beyond abstraction and rather see it in its concreteness. This culminates in a belief in the ability of an aged dead to return to the lineage through a second birth. Names such as Babajide, Babatunde and Yetunde among others provide credence to the Yoruba world of interconnections and interdependences, while also de-emphasising the biological aspect of conception.

Spirits of the ancestors also manifest in the form of masquerades (*ara orun*) who make regular appearance to the world. The fluidity in their manifestation (being corporeal at one point and indiscernible at other times) suggests the Yoruba universe as a complex panoply of incorporating and interweaving dynamics. When the Yoruba ancestors appear in the form of masquerades, they live in the present and form themselves into custodians of morality and regulators of social order. As embodied ancestors, masquerades embed the relationships between the physical world and the hereafter, and hold serious implications for communal stability. Masquerades also adjudicate in intricate interpersonal and group conflicts, invoking both their transcendentalism and the inviolability of kinship ties as elements of enforcing their pronouncements. But even when they occur outside the masquerade form, ancestors are seen as permanently in communion with the living. Achebe's comments concerning the Igbo ancestors, that 'our dead fathers are weeping', (1958, 162) is in this context very apt. Ascribing emotion to the ancestors not only serves to humanise the dead, but also conveys a sense of their presence and interest in the attainment of some sets of culturally sanctioned outcomes. Similarly, Birago Diop, the Senegalese negritude poet, in *Les Souffles*, focuses on the unity of the living, the dead and nature. In 'Spirits', one of the titles in *Les Souffles*, Diop writes:

> Those who are dead are never gone.
> They are there in the thickening shadow,
> The dead are not under the earth.
> They are in the tree that rustles,
> They are in the wood that groans,
> They are in the water that runs,
> They are in the water that sleeps.
> They are in the hut, they are in the crowd.
> The dead are not dead.[6]

It is not in all instances that those who traverse the worlds of the living and the dead are protective of humans. Of course, there are spirit-children (*abiku*) who delight in tormenting mothers through circles of births and deaths, a state Wole Soyinka, in his poem titled *Abiku*, describes as 'coming and going'. Spirit-children, Ben Okri once said, spread 'horror amongst mothers' (1991, 10) and require costly ceremonies to sever their connections with the spirit world. Similarly, there exist the evil spirits of the unburied dead who are ever hungry to do harm to the living (Achebe 1958, 25). Quite unlike spirit-children, their anger is often kindled by perceived injustice meted out to them when alive, or failure of the living kin to perform the transformational rituals required for them to be enlisted in the community of ancestors. Just as *abiku* and angry spirits of the unburied dead are unfettered in terms of spatial negotiation, so too is the Yoruba *akudaaya*, the term that communicates the belief in the dead being capable of a normal life, often in a distant community and away from family and friends. Enjoying a perpetuity not associated with the dead in Christian ethos, the *akudaaya* easily reflects the Yoruba notion of incompleteness, a reality Amos Tutuola captured in his novel, *The Palm-Wine Drinkard*.[7]

Then, there is the idea of a liminal space, mostly conceptualised as a space of in-betweenness. I have chosen to consider this as a transitory terminal and a point of interconnectivity due to its capacity to activate and de-activate itself. While embedded in incompleteness, liminality situates being in a trajectory that can branch off in two opposite directions – forward or backward. It was perhaps this liminal space that the 'palm-wine drinkard' in Tutuola's novel had in mind when he set out to look for his dead 'palm-wine tapster', saying, 'Then I thought within myself that old people were saying that the whole people who had died in this world, did not go to heaven directly, but they were living in one place somewhere in this world' (Tutuola 1952, 9). With such a notion of liminality, Tutuola renders the Yoruba epistemology as introspective and abounding in mediatory techniques. From the 'one place somewhere in this world' decisions are taken that alter the state of being, or convert the supernatural to natural and the natural to supernatural. Although the success of the 'palm-wine drinkard' in locating his 'palm-wine tapster' gives expression to the element of connectedness in the Yoruba reality and universe, his inability to bring him back home appears to limit most instances of interconnections to the terrain of consciousness. But then, there is the usual thought that consciousness is subject to reification, and this much is demonstrated in the magical egg, which the dead 'palm-wine tapster' has offered the 'palm-wine drinkard' in lieu of the 'tapster' returning to the world of the living to continue tapping wine for the 'drinkard' (Tutuola 1952, 120–122). The magical egg takes on the role of the 'tapster', while also performing so many wonders that suggest the interaction between the worlds of the living and of the dead as full of possibilities.

Yoruba posthumous paternity therefore occurs in the mould of what the French anthropologist, Jean-Pierre Warnier, captures in his concepts of 'container kings' and 'piggy-banks'. In these two concepts, Warnier (1993, 2007) offers one of the most comprehensive illustrations of continuities between the world of the living and that of the dead. He describes the container kings of the Cameroonian grassfields through whom ancestors transmit live substances in the form of bodily fluids to ensure the continued reproduction of society and the social order. Warnier (1993, 305) observes concerning transmissible live essences: 'It is the principle of the transformations of beings and material substances into one another, in reversible or irreversible time.' Based on this principle, reproduction is not founded on the biological virility of a man but is rather conferred in a ritual, and tends to be symbolic of an unbroken tie between members of a clan or an entire community (Warnier 2007). With posthumous paternity, the act of conception simply occurs as a social process, a conventional unconventionality of sorts, and a performance of an endogenous value system.

In this book, I move beyond a structural-functionalist notion of posthumous paternity (a perspective common to all views that explain posthumous offspring in terms of the levirate practice) to seeing the custom as one of the numerous ways the Yoruba manifest transformation and as well transform manifestation. If the dead in the Yoruba could see, eat, offer protection to the living, and congregate on the matter of the lineage,[8] then every logic points in the direction of their being alive, perhaps 'in one place somewhere in this world' as Tutuola (1952) rightly observes. In this form, the dead in Yoruba cosmology have an interesting connection with the deities who in the local consciousness are historical as well as supernatural entities. It is in this logic that the idea of a woman's deceased husband continuing in the task of fathering children can be rationalised. A worldview like this, in Francis Nyamnjoh's opinion, 'suggests that death has the capacity to deliver one onto godlike attributes of presence in simultaneous multiplicities, and the capacity to act on others without necessarily being perceived to be present in conventional ways' (n.d). I explore posthumous paternity from this dimension of the dead that are living and argue that their agency, definitely, is one couched within an endogenous epistemology – a thought process that is not subject to external validation, having not aspired toward constituting an imperial epistemology or becoming a universal ideal.

The dynamics of 'unequal encounters'

According to Okot p'Bitek, the greatest challenge to an endogenous African epistemology in the postcolonial era has been the attitude of Africans to their own cultures (1989). The African way of life is quite unfamiliar to many Africans and constitutes the monstrous and a reprehensible path to follow in a world dominated by ideals of Western modernity. In the postcolony, the African reality is realisable more in its spatiality and physical boundedness, the continent having been stripped of its very soul – the languages, belief systems, social and political ideologies, among other cultural apparatuses – and subjected to an epistemological transplant of sorts. Stories of how Africa was raped, decimated, repressed, manipulated and disoriented by the European world (Rodney 1972; Fanon 1967) have proved timeless and ever-relevant to every discourse of the continent's underdevelopment. A core element in the stories is the *missions civilisatrices*, which has been made the justification for colonialism.

Popular stories of the colonial beginning depict the 'whiteman', armed with the Holy Bible as a veritable tool for prosecuting what Amanze (1998, 52-3) describes as a 'war' against African cultures. The Christianity dimension to colonialism was summed up in Thomas Pringle's vision of the European enterprise in Africa:

> Let us enter upon a new and nobler career of conquest. Let us subdue Savage Africa by justice, by kindness, by the talisman of Christian truth. Let us thus go forth, in the name and under the blessing of God, gradually to extend the moral influence… the territorial boundary also of our colony, until it shall become an Empire. (Hammond and Jablow 1977, 44 cited in Mudimbe 1988, 47)

In other words, the Christian's salvation message was not an end, but a means to attaining an end that was as much political and cultural. Chinua Achebe in *Things Fall Apart* is particularly critical of the role European missionaries and their African collaborators played in dismissing the African ways of life. In the assertion, 'But he says that our customs are bad; and our own brothers who have taken up his religion also say that our customs are bad' (1958: 141), Achebe underscores the dismissive European attitude toward African cultures and the supportive role Africans played in denigrating their own value system. Fela Anikulapo Kuti, the Nigerian Afro Beat proponent, once termed the tendency of Africans to sheepishly embrace Western modernity as *follow-follow*. Of course, Africans who quickly bought into the civilising logic of the West by converting to Christianity and acquiring Western education, became the successors to the establishments later left behind by the colonialists. These categories of elites soon became the most alienated Africans on the continent (Rodney 1972, 248).

Christian religion has also played a central role in alienating Africans from their lands and heritage. For example, Bishop Desmond Tutu, in the following quote widely ascribed to him, more or less revealed the hypocrisy of missionaries' salvation theology: 'When the missionaries came to Africa they had the Bible and we had the land. They said, "Let us pray." We closed our eyes. When we opened them, we had the Bible and they had the land.'[9] In a way, the land embodies all that is the African reality – economy, politics and beliefs – including the very idea of the past and the future. Hence, by appropriating the land, the colonial power through the Christianisation process assumed total control over the mind of Africans in terms of what the mind cultivates. Taylor (1963) cited in Mudimbe (1988, 53) puts the salvation theology in perspective by affirming that 'the Christian Faith has for many years…been inextricably bound up with this Western aggression'. This aggression has by no means come to an end, especially with the rigour that has gone into the evangelisation activities of the new generation of Pentecostal churches. I found it significant that the aspect of the church service was omitted from the Ilupeju marriage ceremony that I attended, even though an elaborate church event has come to constitute an essential feature of most Christian marriages in Nigeria.

Institutionalised government has proved to be another effective tool for the suppression of Africa (Achebe 1958). A basic feature of the colonial government in Africa was the legal systems, fashioned after those of the European powers. Where customary laws were recognised, there were legal frameworks that governed their applications (Asiedu-Akrofi 1989). Through such Western-oriented legislation, African subjugation was enforced and resistance punished. As Nyamnjoh (2004, 339) rightly observes, 'Unequal relations of power meant that Africans were forced to comply even when they protested.' Interestingly, a regulated continuance of traditional African law and judicial institutions was permitted in some cases except where they were considered repugnant to 'civilised' ideas of justice and humanity (Allot 1965 cited in Asiedu-Akrofi 1989, 571). In Nigeria, for instance, there were special provisions in the laws of the regions that gave recognition to native law and custom. This, however, was in the area of the jurisdiction of the courts and the applicability subsisted to the extent that such native law and custom was 'not repugnant to natural justice, equity and good conscience nor incompatible either directly or by necessary implication with any written law for the time being in force' (Allot 1965 cited in

Asiedu-Akrofi 1989, 571). With the repugnancy principle, the validity of African customs became tied to the dictates of Western morality. Customs that failed the validity test were prohibited and the African ways were systematically expunged from people's consciousness. Under the regime of proscriptions, people parted ways with a number of their traditional values of kinship, including posthumous paternity, and were absorbed into the world of Western modernity. In Chapter 5 of this book, the unequal encounter between Africa and the West is well illustrated in the ascendancy of ART, a procreation practice, the ideological basis of which is very similar to prohibited posthumous paternity.

The suppression of Africa is not only restricted to the annihilation of its cultural values during the years of colonialism. Francis Nyamnjoh (2004) shows in his analysis of the political economy of academic publishing in Africa that knowledge on the continent is racialised, and Africans seeking universal acclaim are expected to conform to Western intellectual and literary standards. In his words:

> Being published or being read thus becomes much less a function of how relevant to understanding the African situation is a writer, scholar or writing, than a function of how well it suits the purposes of conforming to western norms and expectations. (Nyamnjoh 2004, 334)

Unfortunately, like in the early days of colonialism, African elites are relentlessly engaged in enforcing the rules, which subject the authenticity of every African product to the Western test of validity. In no other sphere is the systematic prohibition of Africa more manifest than in the (neo)colonial education system that de-emphasises African languages and forbids students from speaking them in schools (Nyamnjoh 2012, 140). Of course, it is possible that some readers of this book yet remember the cliché 'vernacular is totally prohibited', which was popular in primary and secondary schools across Nigeria in the 1970s and 1980s. The unfortunate angle to the prohibition was that most pupils then, especially in rural communities, could barely string two sentences together in the English language which was made compulsory as the medium of communication. The stiff punishments following any breach ensured that many minds were silenced and confidences extinguished. For example, students who could not express themselves in the English language usually maintained forced silence throughout school hours. As Schizha and Kariwo (2011, 18) have observed concerning the effect of colonial education on pupils, 'The system filled their minds with abnormal complexes, which dehumanised and de-Africanised them leading to an alienated mind.' A situation in which Africans lost touch with their own and never got to master the foreign, has led to a kind of cultural disorientation, often depicted as conflicts in the works of many African writers (Achebe 1958, 1961, 1964; Oyono 1956, 1960; p'Bitek 1984, 1989; Soyinka 1975).

Following the extant literature on the prohibition of Africa, this book situates posthumous paternity within the larger discourse of epistemicide perpetrated by the West, and shows how posthumous offspring is formed in the sphere for contestation of values. Unfortunately, like in other examples of cultural imperialism, endogenous value tends to have lost out to what has so far proved to be an unequal challenge, considering the level of its exoticness and the resentment drawn from the local community. I, therefore, examine how a decline in the practice of posthumous paternity and the negative attitude displayed toward the identity of offspring flow from a colonial mentality that renders Africa and Africanness inferior and an obscenity. By focusing on offspring's subjective interpretation of their identity, I equally explore the challenges with which African endogenous cultures are confronted when seeking justification and incorporation within an epistemology occurring outside of their very own milieu. As is demonstrated repeatedly in this book, traditional cultural values, wherever they have survived, are exceptions rather than the rule. This, I suggest, accounts for the secrecy that is built around the identity of the posthumous offspring.

Posthumous paternity, levirate and widow inheritance

The concepts of widow inheritance and leviratic unions are important to an understanding of this work. Anthropologists have developed them as frameworks for determining not just the paternity of offspring a widow bears after the death of her husband but also the status of such offspring within the patrilineage. Many works on the African kinship system make allusions to both widow inheritance and levirate marriage as remarriage options open to a widow. In most cases, either the two concepts are used interchangeably (Ebeku 1994; Korieh 1996) or one is projected as constituting the very ideology of a group on a widow's remarriage. This latter approach was common in the anthropological literature on the African kinship system in the 1950s and 1960s (Evans-Pritchard 1945; Radcliffe-Brown 1950; Gray 1964). Rare mentions are also made of societies that practise both, side by side (Ogbu 1978). However, the borderline that separates traditional practices labelled widow inheritance and levirate is not always too clear, and the blur in category might have informed the dearth in the number of scholarly articles that has engaged in serious conceptual clarification, and the tendency of some scholars to equate one with the other.

Both widow inheritance and levirate union were described by Radcliffe-Brown as continuations or renewals of the existing structure of social relations. They are said to be 'examples of the unity of the sibling group since brother replaces brother' (Radcliffe-Brown 1950, 64). It was perhaps in line with this categorisation that Ogbu (1978, 244–245) listed both levirate and widow inheritance as remarriage options that have been reported in different African societies, though he did not distinguish between the two. The fact that older women or those that have passed child-bearing age are most times exempted from the practice associates widow inheritance and levirate especially with younger widows, who are usually the last wives in a polygynous marriage.

A number of scholars, however, explain the difference between the two practices primarily in terms of the identity of a widow's offspring (Radclife-Brown 1950; Gray 1964; Abraham 1976). Concerning this, Radcliffe-Brown (1950, 64) writes: 'In the "true" levirate…the social father of the child is the deceased husband of the mother. In systems of widow inheritance the social father is the present husband of the mother.' Following Radcliffe-Brown, Weisberg (2009, 4) posits that widow inheritance differs from levirate in that the children of the second union are regarded as the children of the new partner rather than of the deceased. Likewise, Simon Roberts, also observing with reference to the customary law of the Tswana, avers that 'A levirate arrangement arises where following a man's death, his widow remains in her *lapa* and has sexual relations with one of his relations with the object of raising children from the deceased' (Roberts 1974 cited in Ebeku 1994, 50). Obviously, the most conspicuous defining feature of the levirate practice has been the ascription of paternity of offspring sired by a levir to the widow's deceased husband. In other words, even when the two practices may involve a widow and the husband's kin relation they are distinguished by the paternity status of offspring. In the case of widow-inheritance, the identity of the deceased is supplanted by that of the successor, whereas in 'true' levirate the opposite tends to take place as the story of Onan and other Old Testament materials well illustrate (Abrahams 1973, 167).

Among the Luo of Kenya, the conception of levirate aligns with the popular notion of the practice, especially in respect of the status of offspring (Oboler 1986; Potash 1986). However, the Luo practice discharges the levir from support responsibilities to the deceased dependants. Betty Potash commented as follows on the Luo's levirate practice: 'Leviratic relationships are characterised by separate residence and widows will typically continue living in their deceased husband's home. Widows have no domestic responsibilities to the levir; the levir has no responsibility for support or socialisation' (Potash 1986, 44). This reality, however, is quite different from that obtained in the Igbo society of Nigeria where the levir has the responsibility of providing social and economic support for the dead brother's dependants (Okonjo 1992; Korieh 1996). The levir in the pre-colonial Igbo society, according to Chima Korieh, was conferred with the normative role of siring children, if the widow's family is not considered complete, among other functions such as managing the property held in trust for her minor sons; assisting her by providing labour for clearing, ploughing, planting and harvesting, and contributing to the maintenance of her household. The Igbo levirate system, Korieh (1996) avers, was an expression of social identification of the kin with one another. The idea of 'true' levirate, which Radcliffe-Brown introduced into his distinction between levirate and widow inheritance, thus suggests variations in levirate practice from one society to another.

Betty Potash has also argued that the levirate relationship of the Luo may be distinguished from marriage, contrary to the most common anthropological treatment of levirate as a continuation of marriage with a consort who acts as the husband's successor. To the Luo, the widow is a *chi liel* or wife of the grave (Potash 1986, 44) and not in any way a wife to the inheritor. But yet, among the same Luo, Kirwen (1979, 3) represents the levir as a substitute for the deceased husband. From Potash's study of the system, it appears the levir is only involved in a copulatory relationship with the widow. Such a role, though important, may not represent or define the normative character of a husband. It is evident that what can appropriately determine whether the Luo practice is marriage or otherwise is the social gap between the levir and the widow. If it happened that no elaborate social and economic support actually flowed from the levir to the widow, as is generally required of the institution of marriage, then Betty Potash might have been justified in her assessment. Interestingly, in Radcliffe-Brown's (1950) estimation, a levirate is more a cohabitation than a marriage.

The distinction between levirate and widow inheritance is also often approached from the aspects of inheritance and succession rights. Generally, in a widow inheritance system, the offspring belong to the lineage of their genitors who also are their social fathers. They are treated the same way as the offspring from a wife a man has married of his own choice. On the other hand, offspring of the levirate practice may not be entitled to inheritance in the household of the levir, but are accorded full rights in and over the estate of their mother's deceased husband (Ebeku 1994, 46). This distinction can become blurred in situations where a levir and the man he has replaced all belong to the same patrilineage, especially in societies where inheritance is through the line of male descendants.

The transposability in the application of widow inheritance and levirate, particularly in reference to the Yoruba, has made it difficult to determine which of the two represents the people's orientation on a widow's remarriage. Forde (1951, 25) attests to the practice of 'widows passing to brothers and half brothers' and the inheritor's responsibility of providing for widows and children. Similarly, Jeremy Seymour Eades (1980, 59) observes that 'In the northern Oyo towns, widow inheritance is still common in the more conservative compounds.' In Ogbu's (1978) classification of widow remarriage options in different African societies, the Yoruba were associated with only widow inheritance. In spite of the generous reference to widow inheritance, there are, of course, works that have reported levirate practices among the people. Oni (1991, 152) alludes to a Yoruba levirate system which serves to provide a widow with a breadwinner and 'to raise offsprings as it is believed for the deceased'. Such cultural practice, he affirms, sometimes creates a situation of rivalry between the man's wife and the inherited widow. Recently, Ademiluka (2003), describing the cultural heritage of the O-kun Yoruba, emphasised the practice where a young widow is inherited by a young man who is a member of the family of the deceased so as to raise children for the deceased. Similarly, Olanisebe and Oladosu (2014) identify the possibility of posthumous paternity in the Yoruba widow remarriage practice, which they described as inheritance. The authors, however, stress that the purpose of Yoruba widow inheritance is primarily to ensure the welfare of the widow within the family, the woman being an inheritance of the deceased, and not necessarily that of raising children for the deceased. These are recent examples that may serve to open new vistas in scholarly discourse on the Yoruba widow remarriage practice.

For many anthropologists, especially those who pioneered ethnographic research in Africa, traditional practices rendering a woman as part of the estate of the deceased in African societies have long been abandoned. Such an attitude perhaps informed Ray Abrahams's description of levirate as 'a popular ingredient in the anthropological stockpot of exotic kinship institutions' (1973, 163). No doubt, the consequences of socioeconomic changes for traditional practices cannot be ignored. But whether they have effected a complete annihilation of endogenous values is another thing entirely. There is always the question of adaptability of values to explore, as this seems more plausible than an attempt at archaeology of kinship practices.

The analysis in this book takes cognisance of the explanations of posthumous paternity offered by the concepts of widow inheritance and levirate (especially within the bounds of their functional arguments). However, I have chosen not to see the duo purely as *raison d'etre* and the most appropriate interpretation of the complex processes contained in the relationship a woman maintained, particularly with regards to the identity of children born after the demise of the husband. I have adopted this position so that other possibilities that exist outside of the well-reported transfer of a widow to the husband's brother or any of the close kin relations can be explored. More precisely, I link up the act of a woman bearing children for her deceased husband to an endogenous epistemology, which offers the possibility for continuous interaction of the dead with the living.

Between identity and identification

The notion of identity as shared has dominated most understanding of the concept in the discipline of anthropology. The reason for this is not far-fetched – the focus of sociocultural anthropology has been the processes taking place between people, whereas identity has conventionally been understood to exist inside each individual. Thomas Eriksen, in this regard, comments thus: 'When we talk of identity in social anthropology, we refer to social identity, not the depths of the individual mind' (2010: 71). This, however, does not mean that anthropologists have never been interested in personal identity. Giving credence to the element of self in identity, Anthony Cohen has observed that 'Societies do not determine the selves of their members. They may construct models of personhood; they may…attempt to reconcile selfhood to personhood. But they have no absolute powers in this regard' (1994, 71). The idea of an individual having a fixed 'essence' often regarded as the person's identity was also rejected by Foucault who rather saw the self as defined by a continuing discourse in a shifting communication of oneself with others. In 'technologies of the self', Foucault suggests different ways by which individuals act upon themselves to produce distinct modes of identity and sexuality. In his view, through self-contemplation, self-disclosure, self-discipline, and other practices and strategies of representing personal ethical self-understanding, individuals can rise above every form of stereotypical ascription.

In analysing the identity of posthumous offspring, therefore, I align with the perspective that tends to emphasise the individual as 'a particular kind of social person' (Grillo 1999, 228). This is for a number of reasons. First, the idea of posthumous offspring as a collectively defined identity can only be sequel to an acknowledgment and public articulation of their reality. But in the context of this research, we are confronted with a custom whose contemporaneous practicality is mostly denied based on its perceived incompatibility with Western modernity and Christian morality. Second, the posthumous offspring identity, at the periphery of social identity where it occurs, does not galvanise bearers into thinking of themselves as united by a sense of shared traits, except when taken as part of a repertoire of worldviews and ideas of the social. Rather, the identity occurs more in terms of what Jean-Marie Benoist once described as 'disconnected singularity' (Benoist 1977, 15 cited in Eriksen 2010, 71). Third, the posthumous offspring identity is also subject to the level of integration bearers attain in their respective lineages. This varies and has produced in posthumous offspring different interpretations of the social space allowed them in the contemporary polity.

Hence, when discriminated against in society, a posthumous offspring has no collective identity to which to appeal, but instead may apply the cultural toolkits he or she has acquired based on life experiences. Where does this leave posthumous offspring? Because a Western epistemology has eroded their authenticity, most posthumous offspring, I argue, are relentlessly engaged in self-making through a process Stuart Hall (1996) defines as 'identifications' – the dislocation or de-centring of the subject. As Hall observes concerning identification, it is 'a process of articulation, a suturing, an over-determination not a subsumption. There is always "too much" or "too little" – an over-determination or a lack, but never a proper fit, a totality' (1996, 3). For example, posthumous offspring in this book have reacted differently to circumstances that tend to dehumanise them. However, because their being is situated in an overarching ideology, it follows that cognisance is taken of the aspects of their identity that constitute a constant. In other words, while I chart the same course as Hall in viewing cultural identities as open-ended, I also explore the unified reaction or consensus of neoliberal subjects against the identity of posthumous offspring.

In Hall's notion of identity as a 'moveable feast' one simply finds an explanatory tool for the state of incompleteness of posthumous offspring. Interestingly, this is not just about them as humans, contending with numerous everyday realities that represent a quest for completeness (Nyamnjoh 2015). A number of their pursuits require that they move between different domains of identity and adapt the self to situational specificities. However, in the case of posthumous offspring, incompleteness surpasses the vision of self-actualisation and also manifests as discrimination and disempowerment. By considering instances when the authenticity of posthumous offspring becomes the subject of dispute, I explore the question of the legitimacy of posthumous offspring in contemporary Yoruba society. The Yoruba believe that the presence of an illegitimate child within the lineage has a disruptive effect on social order and internal cohesion of the lineage. This kind of conviction is most likely to render the identity of posthumous offspring problematic, even within the local community, in addition to limiting the offspring's access to power and many other patrimonies of the lineage.

The analysis I present in this book recognises a particular shade of inequality – the one between Africa and the West, and its expression in the difficult identity of posthumous offspring, or in the dichotomy between Yoruba posthumous paternity and assisted reproductive technology. In every case, we are confronted with the question of portrayal and representation. Hence, I have also explored identity as something that can be imposed by external forces, especially if equipped with instruments of coercion. In so doing, I do not intend to undermine the dynamism of endogenous values, an element of the Yoruba culture that explains the continuous alteration of cultural traits. Rather, I explore resilience within the limits of symbolism, most especially that a resilient cultural practice such as posthumous paternity has assumed new meanings which are imposed on it by an epistemological force with the power of coercion. Yet, resiliency and agency, individual and collective, mean that such zero-sum pretentions of coercive power are ultimately denied the last laugh.

Organisation of this book

This book contains six chapters. The current chapter, Chapter 1, lays out the purpose and motivation for this work which, of course, is the reality of traditional posthumous paternity in the 21st century. Here, I present a wide range of arguments on issues of representations and power relations that are necessitated by the unequal encounters between Africa and the West, the identity of posthumous offspring, especially as it embodied the contradictions in Africanness and Western modernity, the intersection of cultural values across African societies, and the anthropological parallels between Yoruba posthumous paternity and assisted reproductive technology. I review literature on the interconnection and interdependence associated with Yoruba epistemology, the erosion of African cultural values due to colonialism, adaptive kinship practices such as widow inheritance and levirate marriage, and the concepts of self and identity.

In Chapter 2, I provide ethnographic data on the practice of posthumous paternity. The chapter opens with an explication on the culture of secrecy in which the identity of posthumous offspring is shrouded, and the role secrecy plays in the perpetuation of the practice. The chapter then presents an overview of the remarriage options open to the Ilupeju widow and the implications of each for the paternity status of children. Here too, I have focused on a detailed discussion of the status of children born from illicit extramarital sexual relations. The chapter goes on to present narratives from conversations held with four key informants, made up of three posthumous offspring and a 'helper'. These narratives cover how posthumous offspring make sense of and manage their identity within the extended family, how they construct self and relations, and how they achieve integration into the lineage. Finally, the chapter, drawing from the ethnographic narratives, spells out how self is implicated in the posthumous offspring's encounters with their unique identity.

Chapter 3 explores the dynamics of power in the contemporary practice of posthumous paternity, by examining the interplay of identity and power relations in the social, economic and political engagements of posthumous offspring. It analyses the community's notion of legitimacy, and what people consider the real or imagined rights of posthumous offspring to property, land and titles of patrilineage against Nigerian legal provisions on 'fictitious genealogy'. Furthermore, the chapter considers the role of modernity in creating tensions about the identity of posthumous offspring. The chapter further assesses posthumous offspring's access to power and how it influences the rethink of their identity. Generally, the chapter develops its argument around the contradictions entailed in the interaction between traditional and contemporary ideologies of belonging, which it in effect blames for the abridged identity of posthumous offspring. It also explains how conflicts arising from contestations are resolved.

In Chapter 4, I explicate on the authenticity of posthumous paternity as an indigenous kinship practice in the study community and explain its limited notion in the literature in terms of the marginal positions some Yoruba communities, particularly those located in the eastern fringe, occupy in the overall construction of the Yoruba identity. The chapter situates the practice in the context of the unique nature of borderlines, frontiers and crossroads as melting points, facilitators, negotiators, and spaces of contestations, inhibitions and possibilities. The chapter also examines the Yoruba kinship system against current data on posthumous paternity. It explores the lineage structure, the terminology of kinship, and the descent system across the Yoruba dialect groups for traces of posthumous paternity. It discusses how posthumous paternity challenges existing terminologies of kinship and attempts a re-conceptualisation of Yoruba kinship terms and categories to accommodate the reality of posthumous offspring. The chapter also examines how the practice has shaped the Yoruba ideology of belonging.

Chapter 5 draws anthropological parallels between the Yoruba posthumous offspring and children born from cryopreservation of sperm and embryos and other forms of artificial reproduction (AR) or assisted reproduction technologies (ART). It argues that issues of legitimacy and identity are implicated in both cases. The chapter also examines the question of 'help', 'donation', physiological paternity cum biogenetic connection and parenthood that are also rendered problematic in the two cases. It considers the prospect which the knowledge of traditional posthumous paternity in a contemporary society offers for dealing with the sociocultural challenges that may confront AR or ART in the immediate future. The chapter further examines the implications of the repugnancy principle of the Nigerian customary law for legitimation of such practices like *in vitro* fertilisation in Nigeria, especially as it may concern inheritance and succession laws.

Chapter 6 rethinks cultural resilience in the context of posthumous paternity, and examines the challenges entailed in endogenous kinship practices surviving in an environment dominated by Western constructs of family, parenthood and identity. It also explores the dilemma of the African mind in rationalising its endogenous cultural practices and the epistemological debates provoked by cultural survivals. It reviews the existing disposition of local people to posthumous offspring as a way of explicating on the unequal encounters between Africa and the West. The chapter also examines the anthropological lessons that can be learned from the survival of Yoruba posthumous paternity, particularly the implications of the practice for women's empowerment.

Notes
1 Work of Nigerian playwright, Ola Rotimi, and an adaptation of Sophocles' *King Oedipus*.
2 In the matter of Chinweze v. Masi, five justices of the Supreme Court, in a unanimous judgment, ruled that posthumous paternity was repugnant to natural justice. Extensive discussion of this is found in Chapter 5.

3   I follow Francis Nyamnjoh (2012, 136) in adopting endogenous rather than indigenous in categorising the bodies of African epistemologies. Detailed treatment of this concept is contained in his article, "Potted Plants in Greenhouses": A Critical Reflection on the Resilience of Colonial Education in Africa published in *Journal of Asian and African Studies*, Vol. 47, No. 2, pp. 129–154.

4   Most people I spoke to during the fieldwork regarded posthumous paternity as an outdated practice, with which they no longer expect anyone to associate.

5   In their dictum *b'ina ba ku a fi eeru b'oju; b'ogede ba ku a f'omore ro'po* (the ashes survive fire and a banana replaces itself with the sucker) the Yoruba emphasise the continuity of life.

6   The poem was retrieved from (accessed 26 June 2016): www.sage-ing.org/wp-content/uploads/Diop-ThoseWhoAreDeadAreNeverGone.pdf

7   Extensive discussion of Amos Tutuola's *Palm-Wine Drinkard* and the Yoruba notion of incompleteness can be found in Nyamnjoh, F. B. 2015. "Amos Tutuola and the Elusiveness of Completeness." *Stichproben. Wiener Zeitschrift für kritische Afrikastudien*, 15: 1–47.

8   The Yoruba culture, like many other cultures in Africa, humanise the dead, who are regarded as capable of most acts performed by the living.

9   The source of this quotation cannot be officially ascertained, but most mentions of it in online media ascribe it to Bishop Desmond Tutu.

2

The fated grass: Self-representation and identity construction

Any debate initiated on the ascendancy of Western epistemology in postcolonial Africa stands to be a mere academic exercise. Across the continent it is common to have endogenous cultural apparatuses and their aficionados depicted as being off track. For many Africans, Western modernism, seen as progress, has permanently overtaken African ways of life, although there are moments of nostalgic retelling of the endogenous morality often captured as the good old days. Interestingly, surviving elements of African cultures, especially the kinds that Amin describes as 'vestiges of the past' (1974, 377) are constantly required to justify their pertinence and contemporaneous relevance to the very structure that had rendered them exotic and an anathema. In this enterprise, anthropologists – including African academics – are constantly preoccupied with the task of investigating factors that enable resilience, as there seems to be consensus about the unusualness of cultural continuity. This prevailing attitude toward endogenous practices shapes the way posthumous offspring construct self and identity.

In this chapter, I focus on the different ways the Ilupeju posthumous offspring make sense of their identity as individuals, and how self-representation portrays them as the unfortunate compromise of an unequal colonial encounter. Although an element of in-betweenness mostly characterises their notion of self, a sense of an identity is ostensibly embedded in each posthumous offspring's belief that he or she could circumvent, in a unique way, the numerous encumbrances associated with being different. Like many other endogenous cultural practices that have taken new meanings so as to achieve acceptance in the new 'global' order,[1] posthumous offspring's struggle for acceptance in their social milieu is not waged on a specific ideological platform or under a sense of a collective. Instead, it is rooted in the identification each individual considers sufficient to guarantee social inclusion. Interestingly, when the colonial enterprise upstaged the endogenous epistemology, it erected structures of liberalism or neo-liberalism, which promoted individual agency. In this chapter, I explain the lack of a shared sense of identity in posthumous offspring in terms of the burden placed on each of them to negotiate membership of the lineage and participation in its activities under an arrangement that dichotomised social realities in the categories of tradition and modern. Individual's strategies of self-making are therefore not fashioned outside a demeaning compromise, which popular endogenous values make when seeking accommodation from an imperialistic epistemology.

The manner in which posthumous offspring construct self also underscore an epistemological dissonance and a sense of incompleteness on their parts. In other words, a process of self-awareness is not only problematic most of the time, but also constitutes a resource for passive engagement with the social environment. For instance, sometimes, in order to avoid unnecessary interrogation of his or her identity, a posthumous offspring may not be too assertive in contesting space and resources. At other times, other forms of identification are sought to cloak and, in some instances obliterate, what is considered an awkward identity. In this regard, I examine how the posthumous offspring identity creates what Sökefeld (1999, 421) has called 'a separate "compartments" of the person'. An awareness, especially of inconsistency in identity, I argue, underscores the dilemma and confusion often provoked in the African mind as a result of being incorporated into two different and most often, opposing worldviews. In all of this, I have equated the circumstance of the posthumous offspring with the fated grasses, which a popular African proverb posits, bear the brunt of the fight of elephants. The only difference here is that a particular elephant, though weakened and generally believed to be doomed, would not just give in, especially on a turf it considers home. A central subject for this chapter, therefore, is the manner in which the practice of posthumous paternity might have gone underground to evade being totally obliterated by Western modernity. I examine the creative approaches formed to provide a necessary shield to 'fated grasses' that remarkably constitute the most obvious evidence of the resilience of endogenous cultural values.

In Nigeria, the identity question has assumed a major discourse in the area of national politics, as well as penetrating deep down into the local arena, and into every sphere in which resources are allocated and contested. It also forms the basis of numerous instances of exclusion politics practised at all levels of governance. In this book, the assumption that an individual may not legitimately belong to a particular context of claim-making lies at the very heart of the views which most of my informants expressed regarding the cultural practice of posthumous paternity. How individual offspring situates or configures self in relation to others thus constitutes a major focus of this chapter. The ethnographic narratives, which also cover the way they make sense of and manage their identity within the extended family, and how they achieve integration into their respective lineages, offer insights into the complexities embedded in 'being and becoming' in contemporary societies.

In this chapter also, I focus on a detailed discussion of the paternity status of children born from extramarital sexual relations. The understandings in this regard, which emanated from Ilupeju, challenge the most common notions of illegitimate children and set the concept as another field in which 'being and becoming' in contemporary Africa is constantly structured by Western epistemology. While it interests me to see how posthumous offspring contend with conditions of otherness through their individual narratives, the real discourse in this chapter will be found in the way the inscription of self on the posthumous offspring's identity communicates an unrelenting struggle of endogenous epistemology for incorporation within its very own milieu. However, this chapter does not include an analysis of the many notions of the self that social and personality psychologists in particular find important.[2]

(Un)veiling the posthumous offspring

I had settled down for fieldwork in Ilupeju before I realised that the identity of posthumous offspring was a difficult subject to get people to acknowledge and discuss. After a week of fruitless engagements with informants, I reckoned that I was perhaps involved in one of those anthropological exercises which Warren Shapiro (2009) aptly describes as 'ethnographic fantasy' or at best investigating an antiquated traditional practice devoid of a living vestige. Most of my informants would spend time giving me a lecture on the basics of widows' second marriage system practised in the community in the past and how it had been overtaken by Western modernity. At some point I thought I needed no more of what seemed a rehash of the same story by different informants and would sometimes ask a straight question about posthumous paternity and posthumous offspring in contemporary times. Many of my informants denied outright any notion of continuity of the tradition; some acknowledged the practice had existed in the recent past; and only a few suggested posthumous offspring currently live in the community.

Amidst my frustration, I reflected on the implications of talking to a stranger about the identity of a community member, especially when such identity is contentious. I knew it would be difficult to get people to speak on the subject because it could simply be interpreted as giving up the most guarded secret of a lineage or a family. Upon this realisation, I conceded that it would never be easy to get posthumous offspring (that is if they really existed in the community) to narrate their personal experiences. I concluded that the example from the wedding ceremony, which had led to my research, was an anomaly that could only serve as a footnote to a study of cultural change and continuity in a modernising society. Thereafter, I listened more to stories of widows' remarriage options, most especially because they offered some new insights that were slightly different from what the colonial literature presented on widowhood practices in Yoruba society. It was at one of such interview session that a key informant, Alhaji Jamiu, offered a clue to what I came to consider the secret underlining the identity of posthumous offspring.

During this interview, Alhaji Jamiu, perhaps inadvertently, admitted that three of his very much younger sisters were posthumous offspring. When I sought his assistance to arrange an interview with them, he pointedly asked me how I intended to explain to these potential informants the source of my knowledge of their family identity. He insisted that he would not be the link to them and wished me good luck if eventually I ever got to meet them in the course of my research. He said: 'If I took you to them, not only would they be disappointed by my action, but they would as well say that I had never for once told them I would call them bastards before a stranger.' Jamiu was right, after all, and I never got to meet the said sisters throughout the duration of my fieldwork. I confronted other informants about my finding and from then on learned that people were understandably discreet about the identity of posthumous offspring and other unconventional paternity except when internal conflict in the family brought it into the public domain. Jamiu explained the veil of secrecy surrounding the identity of posthumous offspring within the framework of *olaju* or civilisation. In his view, posthumous offspring, though a culturally sanctioned identity in the past had, in the modern era, assumed the status of a problematic identity having been stripped of legitimacy by the dictates of Western modernity. This, he said, had given rise to the secrecy around posthumous offspring which, in turn, has ensured limited mention of the subject in the community, and that offspring, on their part, are not supposed to know about their paternity probably until they found something strange about their identity or someone out there referred to them as 'a butterfly that thinks itself a bird'.

Obviously, the idea of not speaking openly about the identity of posthumous offspring offers a number of suggestions. First, it is an acknowledgement of a problematic identity and an implicit endorsement of the Western construction of legitimacy. It also smacks of a general tendency to renounce African cultural traditions. Veiling posthumous offspring comes under the assumption that they constitute a problem. Yet what appears to drive the silence around posthumous paternity is the imperative of shielding offspring from probable stigmatisation. For instance, Jamiu equated a divulgement of his sisters' posthumous offspring identity with being called bastards. Had he done that, he would probably have thrown them out of an important institution of claim-making or restricted their participation in activities of their lineage. Veiling posthumous offspring, in other words, illustrates how identity constitutes both a factor of disempowerment and a protective guard for ensuring participation in the social and economic order of a community. In the interviews I had with other informants, there were also thoughts on identity concealment as a mechanism for preserving kinship ties. For many, the fewer conversations people have on problematic identities, the fewer the crises that may emanate from identity contestations.

When my informants denied knowledge of the practice of posthumous paternity, they did so with the conviction that the practice belongs to an ignoble past. The visibility of posthumous offspring was perceived to be injurious not only to themselves but to a society that considered itself modern. Many informants referred to families where the practice has survived as uncultured and disconnected from the realities of the contemporary period. Such assertions are, of course, in tandem with the postcolonial narratives in which being urbane is primarily interpreted in terms of professing and consuming Western ideals and values. Civilisation, which is the other buzz word whenever endogenous practices are the subject, thus occurs as the locus providing expression to the consciousness that pertains to Africans replicating both the structural and ideological strands of the West. It is mainly under this quest for authentication that posthumous offspring exist as an unacknowledged reality, even where they have existence. In a way, there is the feeling that people have found it difficult to break away from the past, inasmuch as they love to be modern in the Western sense of the word. However, this ambivalence, rather than validating the identity of posthumous offspring, speaks more to the dissonance of epistemological alignment and shows the complications that are entailed in the metamorphosis of endogenous cultures, especially when driven by extraneous factors.

Being 'born from another man's hands'

Anthropologists, from the early years of their discipline, have developed concepts which they employed in describing different forms of human social and biological relationships. For them, it is usual to define these concepts in terms of certain perceived regularities and basic assumptions believed to have universal or contextual applicability as the case may be. Interestingly, human relationships are never going to be fully defined. For instance, when the ethnographer perhaps thinks a particular cultural landscape is completely charted, new patterns have emerged to be defined. In Ilupeju, the language used to denote a certain paternity mould lends credence to the inexhaustibility of anthropological concepts.

My informants mostly referred to posthumous offspring as being 'born from another man's hands'. Conceptually, there is similarity between the Ilupeju notion of posthumous offspring and other cross-cultural examples of the phenomenon, particularly in Africa.[1] In its simplest form, posthumous offspring are children born through a levirate arrangement and with paternity ascribed to their mother's deceased husband (Potash 1986, 44). However, there are variations in the Ilupeju example that attest to the uniqueness of the paternity practices of the people. For example, the Ilupeju posthumous offspring is not always a product of what anthropologists have described as leviratic union. In this case, the genitor may not actually be someone assigned by the lineage to enter into leviratic union with a widow for the purpose of raising children for a deceased. Nevertheless, paternity of offspring emanating from the union a widow contracted outside an arrangement that is sanctioned by the family of her deceased husband is ascribed to her deceased husband. Such a union could be with the husband's patrilineal or matrilineal kin, or, better still, with a non-kin relation. Under any of these conditions, offspring are said to be born from the hands of their genitors. On the other hand, paternity of offspring of a sanctioned relationship between a widow and her deceased husband's kin relation is ascribed to the inheritor. This second scenario, I am compelled to argue, is a recent development and a detailed elaboration follows in Chapter 4.

The idea that a legitimate child can be born from the hands of another man dominated local views on the concept of posthumous offspring. I was told that once a union with a widow was not sanctioned by the family, the genitor is deemed to have only 'helped' the deceased to raise more children. As such, he has no legitimate claim to the children and would not pretend to be their father, either by way of socialisation or economic support. With this practice, the notion of continuity of a marriage after the death of the husband seems to be indirectly reinforced, echoed in the exact words of an informant: 'There is a clear message that a widow is not without an owner.' The Ilupeju people offer a functional explanation of their paternity ideology, which they consider as a disincentive for men engaging in adultery with widows and a stabilising factor in the lineage system. I have reservations about their explanation since it is arguable whether a deterrent function can be found in a practice that probably discharged a man from his socio-economic responsibilities, which otherwise could have constrained his indulgence in unbridled sexual relationships. Apparently, the functionalist discourse was foregrounded in the notion of a sense of loss a genitor was expected to suffer from being de-fathered, ignoring the aspect of pleasure that may be found in sexual permissiveness.

Being born from the hands of other men has other dimensions. The people also applied the concept to offspring of extramarital affairs or other birth circumstances including that which Filipović (1958) has described as vicarious paternity.[2] In this particular instance, the husband is alive and aware of the facts of his wife's pregnancy but choses to appropriate the offspring. One of my key informants described another extreme where a man may impregnate his brother's wife but would invariably forfeit the child to the brother. He narrated a personal experience involving him and his wife's brother. According to him, his elder brother's wife once seduced him into having intercourse with her. He averred the brother's claim to the offspring in the case of a pregnancy resulting from the intercourse.

Obviously, many of my informants and maybe the community did not regard it as strange that an individual was born from the hands of another man who generally had no paternity claim. The only problem for such individuals according to an informant is that 'many people know about the circumstance of their birth but usually remain silent on it until such time when their interests conflict with that of a member of the lineage'. Thus, the implications, they suggest, may be dire in future, especially when the genitor is an out-group member, since the Yoruba culture consider it inappropriate for an individual to inherit from any lineage other than his or her own. Acceptance into the lineage through any paternity arrangement, my informants were convinced, did not correspond with unlimited rights and privileges. In which case there was an assumed social boundary that individuals of questionable paternity must not cross to remain in good standing with the lineage. Moreover, there was an implied hierarchy of kinship, which subordinated persons born from the hands of other men to other individuals in the lineage.

Illegitimacy, as Hartley argues, involves the absence of legitimacy, although the most important component of it is not a formal law but rather 'the recognition by the social group of the rights and responsibilities of parenthood' (1975, 3). The Yoruba of southwest Nigeria place a lot of emphasis on the legitimacy of a child and would organise ceremonies for a newly born baby as marks of recognition of the lineage membership (Lloyd 1955). Being *omo oko* (legitimate child) or *omo ale* (illegitimate child) is mainly produced by an acknowledgment or otherwise of responsibility for a woman's pregnancy by a man who may not necessarily be a husband. In the pre-colonial Yoruba society, it was normal for a lineage legitimacy ritual to be performed on a child whose paternity was in doubt. To the Yoruba, the presence of an illegitimate child within the lineage has a disruptive effect on social order and internal cohesion of the lineage. A child termed illegitimate may grow up in the household of the mother's husband and is expected to be aware of his or her status. Illegitimate children who perhaps are oblivious of their status are seen as impostors and society in several ways reminds them of their extraneousness if and when necessary. Thus, a woman who has a child out of an extramarital affair is compelled to seek out the man responsible for her pregnancy, with a view to making him accept paternity of the child. Where this proves to be unfeasible, she is expected to send such a child to her paternal lineage for fostering. Moreover, a child presumed to be illegitimate in a lineage can achieve legitimacy in the lineage of whosoever admits to being the inseminator. The full import of these measures is in the people considering it imperative that a child be incorporated into a lineage he or she is connected with genetically. Meanwhile, other than its legitimate offspring, a Yoruba lineage may also be peopled by strangers and freed slaves who have been absorbed into the lineage system by their former masters (Lloyd 1955).

Basically, and in terms of cultural justification, Ilupeju posthumous offspring are legitimate. Although there is the ostensible inconsistency of paternity form, which sometimes corresponds to that of children deemed illegitimate, the cultural interpretation of their being posthumous offspring supposedly exempts them from such mundane characterisation as illegitimacy. In other words, theirs is an identity thought to transcend biological and social borders of the post-incorporation era, and derives more or less from an endogenous epistemology founded upon endless possibilities rather than empiricism. However, with the source of legitimacy withering, an interpretation of posthumous offspring that tends toward illegitimacy is on the ascendancy. Like all other local structures and modes of being that imperial epistemology has dismissed, posthumous offspring existence is in focus.

Ethnographic vignettes: Posthumous offspring and self-presentation

I felt tension develop in me as the prospect of meeting posthumous offspring became real even though it had always been my desire to interview them. Much earlier, I had received third-party accounts, but somehow, I was going to embark on an act that amounts to what the Yoruba would reckon as 'Counting the fingers of a six-fingered man right in his presence.' No doubt, like an average person of my generation, I consider them strange, yet have to figure out how to interview them without making them feel odd. What are the questions I should ask that would not necessarily amount to putting them in the dock? Following the tradition of ethnographic inquiry, I have given thought to reflexivity. Certainly, as a member of the Yoruba ethnic group, I knew I would struggle to remain neutral to their reality – their unshared identity.

Taiwo Idowu[3] is a man in his early thirties. Like all other youths in his community, he had been actively involved in party politics since the return of Nigeria to democratic rule in 1999. Taiwo decided in 2014 to contest the position of youth leader of his political party in the elections at ward level. Before then he had successfully convinced the party stalwarts that it was the turn of his lineage quarter to produce the ward's youth leader. Taiwo, however, was not the only one in his quarter that was interested in the position even though he seemed not really troubled by the prospect of a challenger, considering his grassroots popularity and mobilisation power, all of which he had thought would count to his advantage. The contest turned out to be fiercer than he had initially contemplated and the elders of his quarter at a point intervened to prevent a crisis situation. Unfortunately, Taiwo's ambition ended in an anti-climax as he himself later described to me. Strangely enough, he did not lose the election but had only been prevailed upon to step down to make way for the other contestant. One of the mediating elders had indeed told him that he was not a member of their quarter and should go to his father's quarter if he desired to contest a political position!

For one, it was general knowledge that Taiwo Idowu had been born from the hand of a man who happened to be a maternal relative of the deceased husband of his mother. A senior member of the quarter, in a clandestine manner, told me that a leviratic relationship between his supposed biological father and his mother had not even been sanctioned by the extended family. Another source stated that Taiwo's biological paternity did not even reside with the man to whom it had been ascribed. But none of these would be an issue in Taiwo's life since the culture defined where his paternity resided. He grew up to accept his mother's deceased husband as a father and sees himself as a member of the lineage. His much older brothers that were directly sired by the deceased also acknowledged him as their brother and one of them even sponsored Taiwo's college education. The elder brother, I was told, described the experience of Taiwo at the hands of some members of the lineage as an act of 'dirty politics', which did not represent the true position of the family. In essence, full integration into his 'father's' lineage was considered to have been achieved over the years in a way that raised no doubt about Taiwo's paternity. It was therefore something of a huge surprise for him that his family identity could suddenly constitute a subject of contention and upon which his political exclusion was not only contemplated but in fact made real.

Taiwo's story was a subject of discussion in the community, especially among local political actors, and while a few people sympathised with him, others thought he should do the 'right thing' by retracing his steps back to his father's quarter. His story, however, proved to be more than just about a defeat an individual suffered in his political aspiration. Taiwo's experience reflected the identity crisis in which posthumous offspring are entangled. It brings to fore the element of power relations embedded in most considerations of an identity as legitimate or otherwise. Furthermore, the experience amounts to a challenge to traditional values, and exhibits the tension between continuity and change on the one hand, and, on the other hand, encapsulates the internal contradiction in a culture that couldn't enforce wholly its own norms and values. The implication of the pronouncement on Taiwo's paternity is that he could remain a member of the quarter insofar as he is ready to accept the marginal position he occupies in the scheme of things, especially in matters that concern patrimony.

I interviewed Taiwo on his botched political ambition and he explained what he believed had instigated the comments about his paternity. He said: 'It has never been an issue', referring to his paternity. 'I am over thirty years now and have been a member of this quarter since I was born. All that is now happening is due to politics.' He went on to describe the intricacies of political competition in the community and the unconventional strategies politicians adopted for engineering political exclusion. He said his rival had been intimidated by his popularity and thus bought over a few elders of the quarter with common gifts and they chose to do a hatchet job. Both labelling and stigmatisation, he said, were common features of politics often employed to scare strong, potential aspirants away, but he insisted he was not perturbed. He likened participation in politics to a situation of a person who detested the touch of water playing by the riverside. In his estimation, the same set of people who had questioned his paternity could still sing his praises to heaven tomorrow. He explained his decision to withdraw from the race then as one borne out of his resolve not to be at the centre of any family problem, since the issue was already generating tension among family members.

Taiwo was down to earth as he demonstrated conviction that there was no inconsistency between the way he sees himself and the way other members of the community probably see him. He said he wouldn't be doing anything differently from what he had been doing, most especially now that the whole world knew about the paternity issue. 'Otherwise, what would they say next time?' he asked rhetorically. He, in fact, promised to contest other elections in the future. Even when I was looking all out for traces of pain in him upon which to reach a conclusion about a contradiction in his self-presentation, he appeared to exude an air of confidence and invincibility. Although Taiwo agreed that his political aspirations had opened his identity to contestation, he believed this was not the real basis for his disempowerment.

Apart from what I have heard from other informants, the story of Taiwo's unsuccessful attempt to become the party's youth leader as narrated by him certainly illustrates the interplay of identity and power. But more importantly, in his management of the experience, he demonstrates the individuated self in every identity. Another victim of name calling or stigmatisation might have sobbed, become a recluse or even renounced membership of the lineage and probably sought reunion with the biological father. But none of these, the young man said, had he at any time contemplated. Taiwo told me that his membership of the lineage could not have been a subject of disputation had he been a 'big man'. Whether he was correct in this assertion would be a different issue entirely. While reflecting further on the strength with which he bore his travail and narrated his story, I could see myself gradually agreeing with him that the real import of his disempowerment might not be located in a contested paternity, after all, but rather in some unholy socio-economic alliance

Chapter 2

forged against him, as he claimed. But then, seeing him as operating largely outside of a cultural milieu in which he has authenticity, I thought Taiwo a symbol of a worldview which, though seemed to be on a path of extinction, has continued to struggle for a space in which to survive. Before we ended our conversation, he again reiterated his claim that identity was secondary among factors of political ascendance and could only have emerged as an authenticating device employed by political elites to engage with the common people. All around him, an air of optimism radiated and appeared to have erased the gloom which I had all the while thought enveloped his real self. I admired his courage and self-assertion all through the period our conversation lasted. Whether he was into performance or true to himself, I couldn't say precisely, but there was this look in him that appeared to be saying 'I have made myself clear.'

Tayo Adeola, a woman in her mid-twenties, had lived most of her life in Ilupeju. After her high school education, she attended the state-owned college of health technology where she was trained as a community health assistant. Most people in the neighbourhood called her a nurse. Although she worked as a nursing assistant in a nearby community, she would return home whenever she was off-duty to help her mother who was a small-time trader. Tayo was born six years after her supposed father had died. She also had two brothers born of the same circumstance. The first time I met her, what struck me most in our conversation was the way she depicted herself. In affirming her status as a posthumous offspring, she described herself to me simply as '*omo oku orun*'. The term actually is used in reference to an orphan, but Tayo's mother was still alive. She definitely meant more than what was literally communicated. Whether she was expressing an essentialist notion of her identity or making a mockery of an identity she believed society had assigned to her was not immediately clear to me. But in our conversation, I sensed conviction in her about who she was and how she had become '*omo oku orun*'. She told me she never knew a father in her years of growing up. Certainly, to her, there was no way that her father could be alive. As a teenager Tayo knew that a devious air hung around her paternity. She acknowledged the uniqueness of her paternity and how she was different from her other friends and even family members, though she also adjudged this very aspect of herself as not all that prominent in her everydayness. In other words, her status as a posthumous offspring rarely reflected in her life situations although it sometimes occurred in conflict with other forms of social identity she bore. Tayo narrated how she knew a man who always came to visit the family even though she was not too certain about the relationship the man bore with her mother until she was in high school. She said, as a young girl, she knew that the mother also at different times sent message to 'daddy Eko' (a daddy in Lagos) who would send money and other items, which she and her younger brother needed for school.

Tayo had many ideas about the cultural practice of posthumous paternity and had heard gossip about individuals in the community who had been born from the hand of men other than their acclaimed fathers. She affirmed that learning of one's real paternity from the street could come as a rude shock. I wondered whether I could ask her if she had ever contemplated affirming publicly her connectedness with her biological father. But then she had not in the entire period of our conversation made reference to the man whom she said often came visiting, and had suggested was connected to her mother, as her biological father. Nevertheless, I asked her. Interestingly, she denounced any filial relationship. 'He is not my father. I told you my father died before I was born', she responded quite swiftly. Tayo further said she never felt any sense of deficiency as a result of her paternity status although she had experienced tension internally each time 'the man' came visiting. She couldn't explain the nature of the tension but I suspected a state of psychological denial.

Tayo also dismissed any idea of a long-lasting effect of a contested paternity status on her, simply on the grounds of being a woman. Ordinarily, as a woman she has limited role to play in the lineage and is most likely to be excluded from the politics of patrimony. 'I am preparing for my wedding and will take up another name anytime soon', she said. Tayo appeared very excited about the prospect of marriage and I could see her face brighten up as our conversation wound down. Her view concerning the temporariness of a troublesome identity further illustrates the gender dynamics that play out in the invention and re-invention of the identity of posthumous offspring. The subsidiary position of women in lineage reckoning and their limited involvement in inheritance matters thus seem to be important factors in considering whatever the effects of identity contestations could be on female posthumous offspring. Tayo made me understand that contestation over lineage membership of an individual was basically related to a struggle for resource and unregulated competition for family patrimony among male members. This she said was irrelevant to her.

Even when she did not state it or when she appeared to have played it down, for Tayo, the identity of posthumous offspring has its own drawbacks. Maybe that was why she was enthusiastic about a new identity, which hopefully could resolve her experiences of internal conflicts. Our conversation indeed revealed much more about the symbolic and social aspects of her identity as a posthumous offspring. According to her, 'It's abnormal when one is unlike other people.' She thought many of her friends could not come to terms with the fact of her paternity when they knew about it. Moreover, she had resolved to speak less on it, and only agreed to honour an interview with me because of the high regard she had for the fellow that had introduced me to her. And I knew she was right because I was not really successful with many others that would have been key informants. All the same, I found in the short conversation the idea of the identity of female posthumous offspring having a transient dimension and consequently being less open to contestations.

The wedding which Tayo had spoken about, was conducted during my fieldwork. It was a second opportunity for me to observe the social processes that played out in a wedding that involves a posthumous offspring after the initial experience, which formed the basis of my research. More importantly, I was also much more conversant with the important roles fathers play in Yoruba traditional and civil law marriages and therefore had expected to confirm one or two things about what she had earlier told me of her paternity. The ceremony was done in three phases. These were the wedding eve, the traditional engagement and the solemnisation of marriage in the local government registry. The wedding eve, particularly, was a period of re-enacting some ritual practices associated with marriage in the community. The venue was the residence of Tayo's posthumous father. Highlights of the wedding eve, however, were the series of ritual dances involving the bride or the *ogbolojo* as rendered in the local parlance. Before her friends at some point also joined her in dance, I had been told that the bride's father would also dance at the event. This knowledge prompted me to discuss with my research assistant the possibility of the biological father who was also present at the event stepping forward to perform the dance for his 'daughter'. A wry smile formed on the face of my research assistant as she assured me the man would never do such thing, and that he was just like any other guest. The responsibility of performing the dance, she said, rested on one of the sons of the posthumous father sired directly by him. As predicted, the eldest son of Tayo's posthumous father stepped forward and performed the dance and was well applauded by the audience.

The wedding continued the following morning with the traditional engagement ceremony. The event, which was held in the same venue as the previous night's dance, brought together the families of the bride and the groom. I was on the lookout for Tayo's genitor, but he perhaps chose not to attend this ceremony. About three hours later, the third phase of the ceremony shifted to the registry of the local government council located in the adjoining community which was less than a mile away. I had been there once before, and the memory was indeed fresh. At the occasion, the couple exchanged marital vows and were subsequently pronounced husband and wife according to the statute. The signing of the wedding register by the couple and their parents followed. Although Tayo's biological father was in attendance, it was no longer a surprise to me that her 'brother' and mother signed as witness to the marriage.

Before my encounter with Tayo I had thought of the posthumous offspring in terms of dual kinship identities (an identity shared with the genitor and that conferred by sociological paternity), but the wedding experience had indicated otherwise. The wedding incident perhaps showed that my idea of a posthumous offspring as self-enmeshed in a conflict of identities was probably more imagined than real. But so many things are not the same for those I have interviewed. Being a posthumous offspring may be troubling at least from a psychological point of view but there appeared to be no indication that an alternative kinship identity was contemplated. For instance, the presence of Tayo's genitor at two events of the marriage ceremony, I was told, was not provoked by any notion of filial association with the bride but instead was born out of an intimate connection established with the bride's mother and an affiliation to the matrilineage of the posthumous father. 'He is a member of the extended family and has a responsibility to be present,' my assistant – who also from time to time assumed the role of an informant – had told me.

Can it then be validly concluded that Tayo was not pained by the inability to identify with her genitor? I held back in drawing such a conclusion, although Tayo affirmed as much and appeared not to have missed a father figure during her marriage ceremony. Similarly, whereas there was no evidence to suggest that the genitor demonstrated indignation over his inability to perform a paternal responsibility, that he felt no sense of loss or challenge was also a conclusion I would rather not draw so easily.

Bayo Ilori was born in 1981 to a father who had died in 1979. He was the first of three children his mother begot for a posthumous father. Bayo's genitor was a matrilineal kin of his mother's deceased husband and, I was told, there were insinuations all around that the genitor had probably been engaging in extra-marital affairs with Bayo's mother prior to the death of her husband. I learned that neighbours had also gossiped about the paternity status of his immediate elder brother, suggesting that he too must have been *born from the hands* of Bayo's biological father based on what they perceived as a striking resemblance between the two. Bayo did his primary and secondary education in the community and attended the state university in Ado-Ekiti, the capital city located some fifty kilometres away. He had, however, returned to the community after a one-year national youth service programme, which was mandatory for young graduates in Nigeria, and hoped to relocate to any of the big cities to search for a job. I interviewed him on a number of issues, which were all related to the practice of posthumous paternity in his community. Though a young man, he nevertheless displayed versatility in community history and traditional cultural practices. He was consistent about the notion of his paternity as complex, and strangely he acknowledged the importance of his two fathers to his self-formation. Talking to Bayo, I encountered for the first time a posthumous offspring ascribing any form of recognition to the biological father.

Bayo told me the level of relationship he had maintained with his genitor was such he had thought did not violate cultural expectations and norms on the one hand, and his humanness on the other hand. He agreed he had a posthumous father, and also a biological father who deserved respect based on a number of factors. He identified the factors to include the leviratic relationship between the man and his mother, the natural bond that should exist between a child and the parents, and the cultural obligation toward an elderly person. He said even when his genitor did not offer him any kind of social or economic support, he would continue to show him the respect a father deserved from a child. Yet Bayo had upheld some of the norms built around posthumous paternity, such as his not visiting the house of the genitor, not acknowledging the genitor's offspring as siblings, and not claiming membership of the genitor's household. But, in a way, he showed helplessness about his status. 'One was born into this reality and grew up with it,' he said, in explaining why it was easy to adopt a seemingly contentious identity.

He maintained all through our conversation that he had not at any point been stigmatised by family members on account of his paternity, but then narrated an experience he once had when a bit younger. According to him, he was on an errand for his mother and on the way had a fight with another boy of his age. The atmosphere, he said, drew the attention of people around and while an effort was being made to stop the fight he overheard two elderly women, who apparently were describing the actors in the clash, identifying him as 'the child his mother bore from the hands of Baba Isale odo'. He said he was not shocked by the reason of the paternity ascribed to him, since he already knew about it, but rather by the fact that the whole story was in the public domain. Bayo also spoke of his university education and how it helped shape his notion of who he was and who he would be in future. He said he took a few sociology courses and from there learned about traditional practices including the levirate marriage and widow inheritance. In his opinion, all of this informed his attitude towards his paternity and his resolve to associate with a man whom he said still visits his mother regularly. For example, Bayo told me he had endeavoured to say goodbye whenever he came around and that both of them chat a lot in the house. He was also of the view that he was the closest to him of the three siblings the mother bore from his hands. The reality of the modern day could, in his view, lead to identity crises for posthumous offspring and he thought his generation was perhaps the twilight of the practice. The only thing he would not admit was that he would one day be willing to reunite with his biologicall father. Though much was suggested from his body language, it seemed he would never mention a thing of such.

I asked Bayo if he knew of the story of Taiwo, particularly the aspect of his failed ambition to become a youth leader. He was surprised that I had heard about it and showed reluctance to discuss the subject until I told him I had previously interviewed

Taiwo. In his first reaction, he said Taiwo had brought all the embarrassment upon himself. 'He should have known that it will end that way since in politics people use everything against you,' Tayo said. He reiterated that it has always been a common knowledge in the community that the easiest way for one to know the true circumstance of one's birth is for one to seek a political position. 'That is the only time you will know if the one you claimed as your father actually fathered you or whether your mother conceived you through a different man,' he said sarcastically. From his own viewpoint, the idea of a posthumous offspring being a member of the family would be valid as long as the ambition of a posthumous offspring did not conflict with that of a kin with a better standing in the patrilineage. He said he had ruled out getting involved in party politics or any local contest for that matter, which would consistently remind him, especially in a derisive manner, of the very fact he already knew about himself. For instance, Bayo told me it had occurred to him in the past to start a small farm on a portion of the family land but that he had decided otherwise due to the insult that may possibly follow. 'You don't know when it can come; they may even send a small boy who you are sure does not know about your history to insult you. That it has not happened to you does not mean it can't happen,' he said. Amidst this cynicism surrounding his self, Bayo yet acknowledged his much older half-brothers born directly by his posthumous father and considered them as focused on forging unity among members of the family.

In another conversation with Bayo, we discussed extensively the issue of his genitor's offspring and the lineage, and what he considered as the relationship he shared with them. Although he played down any relationship, he would not rule out what might happen in future. He said he had a faint relationship with them culturally speaking, by virtue of his genitor being a matrilineal kin of his posthumous father. Beyond that he maintained they were not connected and that his genitor's own offspring too were not socialised to see him as a brother or a kin. When I asked if he would still think the same way had the genitor been a very wealthy man, his response was succinct: 'There are borders you don't cross.' And even when it appeared he was close to his biological father, he said no one in the family had ever pinned any meaning to their relationship, at least to the best of his knowledge. 'He is not a stranger, he is well known as a member of the family.' Bayo, however, suggested that the cultural milieu had been changing so rapidly that it had become unrealistic to insist on doing things the old way. This latter part of his submission was ambiguous and I insisted that he shed more light on what he meant by 'to insist on doing things the old way'. He smiled, and said he was only referring to the cultural practice of posthumous paternity and that he felt a child's genitor should equally hold the paternity once he was willing to take up that responsibility.

In sharing his experience, Bayo presented the image of a fellow weighed downed by the burden of conforming to tradition on the one hand and reacting to the reality of Western modernity on the other. The guarded affection he showed toward his genitor, for one, reflects the functionality of an imperial epistemology and in equal vein the dilemma of incorporation. His claims of reconciliation with his paternity circumstance become unsubstantiated in his numerous avowals, and doubtable because he considered change, especially with regards to posthumous paternity, as desirable. This inconsistency of cultural persuasion characterises the overall make-up of the contemporary African mind.

Baba Ojo, a man in his late sixties, was by no means unpopular in the neighbourhood. His conviviality endeared him to the younger ones who simply called him Baba Ojo. He spent most of his time on a normal day on his farm, but would also spare time in the evenings to play *ayo* at a popular spot not too far away from his house. Baba Ojo had two wives and many children, but had also sired three offspring for his late maternal uncle who died in 1982. One of the children was Tayo Adeola, whom I had earlier interviewed. Everyone in the neighbourhood knew about Baba Ojo's intimate affairs with his uncle's widow even when the woman was not officially 'transferred' to him by the patrilineage. I had followed him after Tayo's wedding and eventually met with him at his popular *ayo* place. There, we had several conversations in which he recounted stories not just about his love affairs that produced three children that were not his in the cultural sense, but also the politics of widow remarriage. His belief in traditional cultural practices was unwavering and he complained about the pressure from Western modernity.

'What I did with my uncle's widow was a standard practice in the past.' He was actually referring to their unsanctioned affairs. The man explained that the interest of the elders of the family on who should inherit the widow did not, sometimes, align with that of the widow. 'But you know women can make anything happen if they are interested in you,' he said, suggesting that he was preferred by the widow ahead of other eligible suitors. He said members of his uncle's patrilineage were not really happy about the relationship, but that whatever complaint could have arisen about their union was rendered irrelevant upon the understanding that he was entitled to the widow. Baba Ojo said he had married his first wife before then, and that his families thereafter had never been threatened by the relationship except a few times when his wives derided him with the *oko opo* (husband to a widow) label. He regarded such an act as an 'unnecessary show of jealousy' and explained that it was normal for women.

He had seen all three children grow up in the community but never once referred to them as his children. In his estimation, such a disposition did not indicate the absence of love toward them except that the love was not the usual fatherly love. He said he had always wished them well as children of his late uncle and never failed to identify with them whenever the opportunity had arisen. He then made allusion to the wedding ceremony of Tayo to buttress his point. According to him, that was where the relationship between him and the three children ended. In his opinion, it was not his responsibility to offer them any form of economic support and he did not pretend to have offered any in the past. 'They have elder brothers (from their posthumous father) who are supposed to do that for them,' the man had observed. However, he had extended financial assistance to their mother and at different times presented her with some harvests from his farm. Provisioning such support, he said, was not mandatory, and must not be evident as it could instigate crises within his own family. 'You know women; they will accuse me of feathering another person's nest,' he said with a cynical smile.

Baba Ojo also spoke about the tension which being the genitor of posthumous offspring could generate if the relationship was not well managed. This he connected to recent transformation in the local tradition as occasioned by *olaju*, modernisation ideas. According to him, the fact that a practice which had not been conflictive in the past could suddenly become a subject of derision and scrutiny was evidence of how much society had changed. He told me he knew that people gossiped about him a lot, even though that had not influenced him to contemplate reviewing what he considered was the 'true' connection he had with the children he sired for his uncle. In the last conversation we had, I asked him pointedly if he ever had cause to regret his act of siring offspring that bore no social affiliation with him. Baba Ojo simply told me to infer an answer from all he had said during our conversations. For him, he had acted based on tradition and had remained steadfast to the cause of tradition.

Picking up the pieces of a broken self

Some forms of identity are cultural capital, others are liabilities. People naturally embrace social categories that empower them while they play down those considered problematic. The manner in which the trio of Taiwo, Tayo and Bayo responded to the reality of their individual identity shows lack of a consensus on the functionality or dysfunctionality of posthumous offspring as a social category. I am compelled to view this as indicative of the force of self that is contained in the social definition of identity. Taiwo demonstrated the zeal to overcome a sense of limitation wrapped with being a posthumous offspring; Tayo's indifference to similar social category was driven by her notion of the role which gender could play in identity negotiation; while Bayo maintained a middle course laced with subtle protest against established cultural boundaries. In the conversations with the three, 'we-ness' of identity was clearly missing and there were indications of self-management. Few works have examined the subjective aspect of individual's experiences and how this has questioned the most popular notion of identity as shared. But the ethnographic accounts so far presented have offered compelling explanations and insights into how individuals can impose their selves on a form of identification that is thought to define the personality of the bearers. Although not independent of the social processes that cultivate an individual, the self, using Sökefeld's (1999, 424) words is 'that reflexive sense that enables the person to distinguish self-consciously between himself or herself and everything else'. It is the factor of difference, which accounts for variation in decision making when people are subjected to similar experiences.

The accounts which the first three informants provided of their experiences as posthumous offspring illustrate the strength of individual differences in confronting a troubling identity. The notion of difference, reflexivity, autonomy and minimised agency is clearly embedded in their interpretations of selves, kin relations and the cultural norms constructed around their identity. For instance, both Taiwo and Bayo, by dismissing the idea of their being restricted to a social space, had perhaps built on the neoliberal ideas of freedom and choice to demonstrate a transcendental self, although Bayo had appeared undecided in his oscillation between a conforming role and protesting against orthodoxy. The individual accounts also show the self as capable of transforming an identity, though not in the sense of altering the facts of identification but in limiting or reinventing the social effects of identity and the idea of identity being a determining factor of human behaviour. Here, the organising role of the self is found in the variegated views expressed by informants about either the relationship they bear with their genitors or the influence they thought being a posthumous offspring exerted on their personal aspirations and drive for honour. Taiwo would not be forced out of politics even when his family identity had been questioned, whereas Bayo would not venture into any contest for the fear of his identity being called into question. It is definitely within these differentiated reactions that the self is expressed.

Poole (1994) provides insight into how the family offers 'the context, the model and the means by which key understandings regarding personhood, selfhood and individuality are learned and internalised by children' (cited in Rew and Campbell 1999, 17). This of course applies to the normal process of enculturation, in which children are supposed to build an identity based on experiences garnered from their immediate environment. In the case of the identity of posthumous offspring, however, there is nothing to suggest that the family makes a conscious effort toward conditioning behaviour in a particular way, especially since the identity in question is not often publicly subjected to scrutiny in a way that specific patterns are formulated. In other words, rather than think of a predictable and shared response to social situations based on socialisation experience, posthumous offspring in their engagements with daily life realities are characterised by individuated rationality, which derives from an interpretation of particular events in relation to the self.

Notes
1. Here I have in mind festivals and cultural sites, i.e. masquerades and shrines that have been stripped of their many aspects in order to be converted into objects of economic production.
2. The cultural practice of posthumous paternity is documented among the Igbo of southeast Nigeria, the Luo of Kenya (Potash 1986), and the Tswana of Botswana (Roberts 1972) among others.
3. In 'Vicarious Paternity among Serbs and Croats', Filipović (1958) denotes a practice among the Serbs and Croats of defunct Yugoslavia whereby the wife of a sterile husband temporarily has intercourse with another man solely in order to become pregnant for her husband.
4. Personal names used in reference to posthumous offspring are pseudonyms.

3

Posthumous offspring and the politics of legitimacy

The story of the failed political aspiration of Taiwo related in Chapter 2 simply provokes some fundamental questions about being and becoming in contemporary Yoruba society. For instance, what are the implications of the illegitimacy 'toga' the identity of posthumous offspring now wears? Under what condition is otherness produced in local imaginaries and everyday encounters? Such questions communicate the very dynamics of the identity construct and intercept with the dominant discourse of a demonization project of endogenous epistemology. By dynamics of identity I mean the subtleties and sensitivities of identity conceptualisation. The first time I learned of the practice of posthumous paternity in a Yoruba speaking community, one of the few things that had me worried then was the extent of integration that offspring could achieve within the extended family, bearing in mind the strong lineage system practised by the Yoruba. My concern was further exacerbated by the centrality of belongingness to the local ideology of claim-making, especially with respect to modern political participation and resource utilisation.

Identity politics in Nigeria often manifest in the notion of the 'son of the soil', which frequently necessitates a superfluous inquisition into the family genealogy of the people aspiring to political positions. Even when the country's Constitution has clear-cut requirements for electoral participation, the unwritten law on indigeneship has proved enduring in Nigeria. As I have argued elsewhere, the penchant for identity politics is driven by a notion of electoral competition as 'turn-taking', wherein competitors are more or less representatives of an ethnic group, community and lineage that considers itself entitled to a particular political office (Ololajulo 2016). Under such circumstance, participation in the political process is based on the ability of an individual to establish a kinship connection to a primordial constituency, which has constituted an informal space of competition, so to say. The idea of political zoning that is implied in electoral competitions thus encourages a terse definition of eligibility and of lineage membership.

Shortly before I completed my fieldwork, Taiwo's immediate family experienced an internal crisis that threatened to disrupt all that the practice of posthumous paternity represents. Prior to the squabble, which became tenser toward the end of 2014, the family was a classic example of the practice of posthumous paternity. Taiwo's mother, Aduke, had lived under the same roof with Wule, the first of the two wives of Taiwo's posthumous father for over thirty-five years after the death of their husband, and during this period Aduke had conceived three children, including Taiwo, for her deceased husband. Though there were a few instances of quarrels between the two wives, which was normal in a polygynous arrangement, Wule was the more motherly figure to Aduke who I learned had actually become widowed just after she'd had her first child. One such quarrel happened in the early years of their widowhood when Aduke accused Wule of discouraging her eldest son from remarrying her.[1] An informant who was very close to the family told me that Taiwo's mother, who then was very young, had thought she would be remarried to Wule's first son who then lived in Lagos, and was really angered when she was rejected. She had only recently forgiven the man, I was told. By and large, however, the two wives had since then lived peacefully in their deceased husband's compound.

In 2014, one of the two daughters of Wule, named Rhoda, purportedly discovered a plot by Aduke to bewitch the most successful of her direct siblings.[2] According to the story, Rhoda, by chance, saw a photograph of her brother in the house of a juju man who, in turn, mentioned Aduke as the source of the photograph. Meanwhile, Rhoda informed her other siblings (excluding the children of Aduke) of the unusual discovery she had made. In another twist to the story, Aduke was said to have accused Wule of employing diabolical and mystical powers to take away the *kadara* (an inherent capacity for prosperity) of her son and embed the same in one of her own children (most probably the one at the centre of the bewitch story). She confronted the senior wife to demand that she return her son's fortune. While still doing fieldwork, I learned that Aduke's eldest son had actually fallen on hard times. The claims and counterclaims created a wide gap between the children of the first wife and their father's posthumous offspring and, at one point, led to a temporary relocation of the first wife away from the family compound. The family crisis moved from bad to worse and Rhoda, in an instance of quarrel, reportedly accused the step-mother of populating the lineage with illegitimate children. She threatened to announce to the public in due course the real paternity of her father's posthumous offspring if Aduke would not stop being belligerent. In this, she had the support of some of her siblings, who thought they'd had enough of the troubles of Aduke and, as such, were willing to sever kinship ties with their father's posthumous offspring.

Meanwhile, the family's eldest son, I was told, did not share a similar sentiment. He was said to have complained about Rhoda's unwholesome utterances and swore not to allow her to 'divide the family' while he was still alive.

The above story, especially with regards to the attitude of Rhoda, exemplifies popular thinking about the question of the legitimacy of posthumous offspring and their positions in the lineage. It, in a way, illustrates both a perception of endogenous practices as outdated, and the feelings that they could have existence only by accepting a marginal position within the very modern milieu. In portraying the positive stance of the eldest son to his father's posthumous offspring, for instance, the story offers glimpses of continuity and support for a beleaguered practice. Above all, it also depicts the interplay of economic dynamics and legitimacy, and how the two enhance visibility, authenticity, and the position of power of individuals within the extended family system.

Salient to my concerns about legitimacy and authenticity is Rhoda's threat to unveil the paternity of her posthumous offspring siblings, thereby rendering them not just of phoney identity but also as indebted to the children of the senior wife for the social legitimacy that they enjoyed. For her, posthumous offspring, much like other forms of traditional culture, constitutes an obscene, trivial and unnecessary burden that has no place in the modern context. But she was not alone in thinking of posthumous offspring in this way. The mentality seems extensive, especially when most people deny that posthumous offspring is still practised. My focus, therefore, is on how the local community treats the question of legitimacy and relates to posthumous offspring in their everyday construction of norms and misnomers. The notion of legitimacy treated here occurs outside of the definition of formal laws and, instead, entails the social space that is allotted people who are assumed to have a problematic identity, particularly when they attempt to access the political, economic and social resources of their communities. In actual fact, I am attentive to how specific meanings about legitimacy are produced from different interpretations and conceptions of posthumous offspring.

Power as an important force in the social construction of legitimacy and illegitimacy is critical to the explanation I make in this chapter. Power in my view here exists in terms of three possessions: *ola* (wealth), *oogun* (juju) and *ipo* (position of authority).[3] The Yoruba reckon the three (severally and collectively) as capable of conferring respect, prestige, awe and invincibility on people who have them. These possessions, understandably, are scarce, and exclusionary strategies are often employed in the processes leading to their appropriation. Such strategies sometimes necessitate defining in- and out-group members. However, the ability of a person successfully to acquire any of these forms of capital can prove essential to the conferment of social legitimacy. And while these resources may constitute the patrimony of a lineage, they can also be acquired independent of the descent group. This chapter explores the role that power, especially in the above forms, plays in either the achievement or denial of legitimacy of posthumous offspring.

It should be of interest here that the people of Ilupeju consider their community to be a unique experiment in settlement amalgamation, at least within the Yoruba context. They see the integrative process that birthed the community as manifesting in an uncommon generosity often displayed by indigenes, especially toward strangers. Although I could neither confirm nor disprove this popular assertion, I am aware that most other Yoruba communities make a similar claim, which is rendered as the explanation for Yoruba urbanisation history which dates back to the pre-colonial era. One of my informants, who acknowledged the reality of posthumous paternity in the community, claimed that continuity of this practice of munificence towards outsiders, as well as their receptive attitude toward posthumous offspring, are both situated within a tendency for accommodation, which he considered to be inherent in the very ideology underlying the establishment of the community. I have listened to him recount the story of the amalgamation, but I found it far-fetched to link it up with the existence of posthumous offspring considering that the much talked about amalgamation only happened many years after the practice of posthumous paternity had been outlawed by the repugnancy doctrine, the details of which I provide in Chapter 5. No doubt, the remarkable story of a settlement formation might be veritable ground to explore other aspects of unusual cultural practices. But then, the connections for now appear vague and insufficient to explain the processes of constructing socio-spatial boundaries in which the legitimacy of posthumous offspring is implicated. In other words, I am indeed concerned about the borders of otherness, the frontiers of legitimacy, where being and becoming appear to be defined ideas of personhood that are somewhat neoliberal in nature.

Analysis in the chapter dwells mostly on informants' views on what the community considers the rights of posthumous offspring in historical and contemporary contexts. This covers rights to inheritance of property, land and titles of the lineage. Interestingly, access to political offices is widely thought to be guaranteed through the lineage under an arrangement best described as political zoning or power rotation at the very micro level. During my fieldwork, there were references made to individuals who have been limited in their aspirations or deprived of accessing a patrimonial resource on the basis of paternity questions. Examples will be drawn from them in the course of this chapter. However, most analysis will be based on Taiwo's story, which was explored in the preceding chapter. Not only was the story recent and compelling but was severally cited by many of my informants.

Chapter 3

Borders of legitimacy

Ilupeju is a peri-urban area by Nigerian standards, although the community can only boast limited public infrastructures that can engage the services of young educated men and women. The most important assets are farmlands. In my early days in the community, I spent time talking with a number of young men about the opportunities open to them in their birthplace. Apparently, many could not see any, and were always planning to leave the community so as to seek employment in bureaucracy or corporate institutions located in cities. Samson, one of the young men who made it a habit to spend time with me, simply said that there were no economic opportunities or other assets to make any ambitious young man think of staying back in the community. Hence, despite this façade of rusticity, it is apparent that there could be very real serious internal competition among community members for the resources below the surface of this rustic illusion.

Contrary to the image of a rural community painted during those conversations, it seems interest in land has intensified since 2011, following the siting of a federal university in Oye-Ekiti, an adjoining community. Not a few people thought that the price of land doubled afterward, especially with the growth of investments in privately owned students' hostel accommodation. Although massive development of properties in the town was at best speculative at the time of this study, there was a benign optimism that made it a matter of time before Ilupeju started benefitting from the emerging economy of a nearby university. Much of the assurance also rested on a notion of Oye-Ekiti having limited land area for infrastructural projects. Moreover, people had heard the stories of how the establishment of the earliest Nigerian universities led to a boost in the economy of the host communities. My friend, Samson, at one point advised me to buy a few plots of land in the community, as he was so sure that I could make a handsome profit from reselling them in the near future. Whether the kind of transformation envisaged would ever happen was not of primary interest to me. Far more important and particularly pertinent for me and for this study is the new consciousness that has grown around land as an economic good and a resource for infrastructural modernisation. Such advancement cannot but have serious implications for local resource rights and raises several fundamental questions. How does legitimacy of individuals intercept with the idea of resource rights and patrimony? How does resource scarcity transform the legitimacy of posthumous offspring? How do neoliberal goals help in destroying the very basis of endogenous values?

In the interviews with informants I sought answers to these questions. Such answers I think can be reasonably valid only when perspectives of the ordinary people regarding the social positions of posthumous offspring are treated not as contextually sacrosanct but mostly as representative of a particular mode of thinking. I also find it important to consider contemporary mode of thinking as historically produced. For one, the practice of seeing access to resources or patrimony as framed around some sets of rules bordering on membership of a group tends to be universal. But legitimacy, while occurring within the labyrinth of popular approval, is also entangled in a process of spatial and temporal contestations. Thus, each of the who, when, how, and where questions of legitimacy is pertinent in relation to a particular epistemology and can only assume significance in the interplay of power relations, cultural change and resilience. From what I got to learn during my fieldwork, the legitimacy question of the Ilupeju posthumous offspring is real. It may not have arisen in the past. But then, the local ideology of being and becoming currently requires people to adopt a new configuration and conception of self and relatives. Of course, the Western lens that had since become the dominant mode of visualising self also made it possible for people to (re)construct new forms of Otherness.

The concept of legitimacy was well applied in the various discussions I had on resource rights and patrimony. Nearly all my informants used the words legitimate and illegitimate in denoting rights to lineage patrimony. Their views resonate with the basic notions of legitimacy as empowering. The informants laid out a number of issues such as order of legitimacy, limits of resource rights and sanctity of inheritance through patrilineage. For instance, differences are constantly made between patrilineal and matrilineal kin in terms of their access to patrimony. The views also show recent contestations of the identity of posthumous offspring as premised both on the reality of economic and political resources as scarce and the need to structure patterns of distribution. There has also been the question of a cultural practice as reprehensible. In all, there are at least three themes under which the legitimacy and, by implication, the resource rights of posthumous offspring are discussed in the public space. First is the issue of lineage authenticity, which may be the patrilineage, the matrilineage or, sometimes, neither of the two. The second tends toward a religious explanation and dwells on spiritual questions provoked by questionable paternity. The third theme connects to the personal worth of offspring. This is usually in terms of social status and economic standing.

A major challenge I had in the course of the study pertains to the definition of legitimate children. Most conceptualisations, especially those rooted in the Western line of thought, would refer to children born when there is a valid and subsisting marriage between the father and mother. However, in some African societies like the Yoruba, the factors of valid and subsisting marriage are mostly irrelevant to the social position of a child within the lineage. Rather, the legitimacy of a child is basically conferred by paternity status, by which I mean a man's admittance of responsibility for a pregnancy. In the case of posthumous offspring, the kinship ideology that produced them defines their legitimacy in terms of the locale of inheritance rights. For instance, historical accounts on the levirate practice across many African societies represent resulting offspring as legitimate children of their mothers' deceased husbands (Ebeku 1994).

In cultures across Africa, it might seem that the idea of legitimacy, though primarily biological, is intricately interwoven with the politics of lineage membership, or what I consider to be a political economy of lineage identity. The assumption is pervasive of lineage as an expansive construction, and as such, though organised around some specific norms, yet permits intrusion and accommodation. This applies to the Yoruba lineage system, which is basically patrilineal. But in many other instances, the Yoruba lineage system may incorporate maternal relatives and even strangers and liberated slaves (Lloyd 1955, 241). In principle, admittance into the lineage carries with it legitimacy and an understanding of access to patrimony. However, there is also the notion of legitimacy as either absolute or relative. I was told that no one could 'narrate history' for a lineage member who descends from the male line of the lineage founder. The same may not apply to other individuals whose membership was subject to negotiation. One of my informants described such lineage members as those 'flying with one wing'. The idea of legitimacy as occurring in a spectrum resonates mainly in discussions of patrimony.

Within the scope of what informants described as the traditional context, posthumous offspring exercise inheritance and economic rights comparable in all respects to those that are applied by other children directly sired by a posthumous father. However, in postcolonial times, they appear to occur within the contradictions inherent in the struggle between tradition and modernism on the one hand, and cooperation and competition on the other. In order to understand how the legitimacy of posthumous offspring has been constructed in time, I interviewed a number of informants on their attitude toward the practice of posthumous paternity and, in particular, their notion of offspring. Mr Ebenezer, a retired school teacher, whose views on the practice, I would say, exemplifies the very ways in which the notion some Africans have of the continent's past is blurred by their encounters with Western values, had this to say:

> In the olden days our culture permitted a lot of things that we can now see as perversions. Thanks to Christianity which makes us see things in new ways. I can tell you that the tradition by which widows continue to procreate for their dead husbands was abandoned in this community long time ago. So, any family that has continued it should be the one to provide explanations on why they are swimming against the tide of time.

Mr Ebenezer's scrutiny of posthumous paternity, no doubt, draws largely from his Christian faith. However, by shifting the burden of explanations for the phenomenon to families where the practice has survived, not only did Mr Ebenezer raise himself and the community above endogenous cultural forms but, indeed, suggested resilience as akin to backwardness. In view of the strong influence of Pentecostal Christianity in the southern part of Nigeria, especially starting with the Aladura movement of the 1920s and 1930s in Yorubaland,[4] it is not surprising that Mr Ebenezer harbours such strong anti-endogenous culture sentiments. His idea of human progress and maybe degeneration too, show, I think, how powerfully Western epistemology is entrenched as a mode of thought among Africans. In the course of my fieldwork, I was tempted at different times to respond to the ways informants such as Mr Ebenezer represented the African past, but each time restrained myself from obstructing the local mode of social construction which I intended my work to capture.

From the conversations I had with other informants I found that the identity of posthumous offspring occurs in the realm of what Mosse (1999, 64) has described as 'subordinate social identities'. In the real sense of it, the identity is not widely expressed or discussed and is known mostly only by the few bearers after they might have suffered one form of social exclusion or another. It is a silent identity. Although it is not bound to labour exploitation and dependency like that of the 'untouchable' identity in India demonstrated by Mosse (1999), or overt stigmatisation in the manner of the Osu caste of southeast Nigeria,[5] posthumous offspring identity in the postcolonial Ilupeju community is expected to be expressed in an ambience of self-subordination and emotionless passivity. These strategies of the self, I was told, were essential tools by which good standing in the lineage can be maintained. Self-subordination, according to an informant, refers to the conscious effort of the posthumous offspring to stay away from controversy by avoiding competition and antagonistic behaviours.

Informants' views on the legitimacy of posthumous offspring are also mostly aligned to the widespread perspectives of social change and value transformation in a spatial-temporal order, which Mbembe (2001) describes as postcolony. Quite a number of the people I spoke to (especially older informants) see the practice of posthumous paternity as having been valid in the remote past but as a possibility too unnatural to contemplate in a modern society. Most of them, in the same manner as Mr Ebenezer, described it as a 'culture of the past'. However, a few others interpret legitimacy in terms of the limits of the economic rights exercised by posthumous offspring within the lineage. This category of informants struggled to convince me during our conversations that offspring with questionable identity were not usually discriminated against in terms of access to lineage patrimony, such as farmlands.[6] One of them spoke of a posthumous offspring who collected rent on a property owned by the 'deceased father' without any objection from the brothers who lived in Lagos. Another informant narrated how a young man, whom he described as well-known to have been born from another man's hand, exercised almost a boundless control over the father's farmland because other siblings had shown no interest in farming. Informants also hinted at the complexity in labelling anyone as illegitimate and the inevitability of rumours and sometimes subtle protests about the identity of some individuals within the lineage. This they claimed emanated from erosion of traditional norms and values of self-restraint. Even when most views would suggest some complications in the popular image of the posthumous offspring, only in few cases were they expressly termed illegitimate. It appears people were particularly careful in describing posthumous offspring as illegitimate children.

The positive outlook that some of my informants have of posthumous offspring may signify legitimacy of sort. But does this reflect the reality in the sphere where contests arise over rights to family patrimony? A key informant, Yinusa, while echoing a notion of relative legitimacy, described the space allowed a posthumous offspring as varied and dependent on how a particular lineage was organised. He explained that in some families, posthumous offspring sired by a matrilineal kin relation of the deceased were fully involved in every decision-making process of the lineage inasmuch as they 'know their boundaries'. By this he has meant the readiness of posthumous offspring to accept an inferior status in the lineage system. In other words, acceptance into the lineage through any paternity arrangement, some of my informants were convinced, did not correspond with unlimited rights and privileges. In principle, people believe that offspring of the genuine levirate system have unlimited access to the lineage patrimony, whereas the same cannot be said of products of extra-marital affairs. In which case, there is an assumed social boundary that individuals who are a product of paternity practice thought to be unconventional must not cross to remain in good standing with the lineage. In other words, there is an implied hierarchy of kinship which renders a set of posthumous offspring subordinate to other individuals in the lineage.

The sentiment about a supposed order of legitimacy is dominant in informants' representation of the Ilupeju posthumous offspring. Where exactly within the structure of legitimacy is the boundary of the resource rights of posthumous offspring then located? And what happens when boundaries are compromised? The most likely inference that can be drawn from Yinusa's assertion is simply of abbreviated resource rights for posthumous offspring. Here, the story of Taiwo readily comes to mind. As one informant told me, it was not as if Taiwo's rights to aspire to the position of youth leader was contested because he was not a member of the lineage. Rather, it was for the reason that a supposedly higher ranked member of the lineage was interested in the same position. Taiwo, for one, was born from the hand of a maternal relative of the mother's deceased husband. In other words, what Yinusa described as the act of posthumous offspring knowing their boundary, may also have implied a relative integration, which only comes to be evident when a struggle for a resource ensues between a posthumous offspring and kin relations assumed to be of better standing in the lineage. As Yinusa said of his posthumous offspring sisters:

> They are legitimate children of my father and I believe no one in the family has ever seen them as different. But sometimes, I have this feeling that they restrain themselves from certain family discussions and activities. By this, I am not saying that they show themselves as inferior to any other members of the family.

Yinusa, it seems, was not quite sure of the social standing of his sisters, even within the family. The ambivalence strikes at the very heart of the complexities inherent in the definition of self in a contemporary environment marked by conflicting epistemologies. While Yinusa's feeling does not necessarily amount to reality, it may communicate his very inner consciousness and reflect the actual imagining of his sisters' identity.

A few conclusions can be reached here. The idea of legitimacy as layered or multifaceted suggests posthumous offsprings' social and economic rights as open to negotiation and defines their identity as subject to multiple social relations – some approving and others precluding. To all intents and purposes, relativised legitimacy stands as a clear example of how kinship relations and relatedness among Africans have been redefined following various colonial encounters. It also tallies with the most dominant idea of zero-sum competition promoted by Western epistemology, especially the religious wing, which has constantly shown itself to be intolerant of opposing spirituality. In all of this, there is also the need to contend with the conceptual ambiguity surrounding examples of unconventional paternity, as this has been found to sometimes complicate the interpretation of inheritance and resource rights of individuals. For instance, popular usage of 'born from the hands' tends to blur the difference between traditional posthumous offspring and children born of adulterous relationships who are integrated into the families of their mothers' husbands. Although in either of these instances the suggestion of unusualness may constitute the basis of social alienation, the idea of connectedness is never the same, and socio-economic rights of offspring are negotiated, based on a perceived order of legitimacy.

Legitimacy and the identity of power

In the years following return to civil rule in 1999, political office has emerged as one of the most important resources in Nigeria. Individuals who got elected or appointed into positions are generally revered in their communities due to the sudden wealth they usually acquire and the role they play in clientelist (re)distribution. Aspiring

Chapter 3

office-seekers and grassroots politicians are also well complemented with titles such as 'honourable' and 'leader' in acknowledgment of their elite status. A growing consciousness of political positions as a source of power and a platform to achieving upward social and economic mobility, I suggest, assists local communities in defining political offices as patrimony, the access and utilisation of which must follow existing traditional patterns of resource allocation. In enforcing this logic, local communities in Nigeria frequently form themselves into an opposition to the ideals of Western democracy by engaging in practices that discourage open competition. For instance, an emphasis on lineage membership as a criterion for political participation depicts the relevance of identity locale to the whole enterprise of exercising power.

Interestingly, a recurring feature of Nigerian democracy has been the cry of political marginalisation by various ethno-regional groups. By marginalisation, Nigerians would mean the inability to have a member of their group occupy certain strategic political positions, especially the presidency. Rueben Abati, a frontline Nigerian journalist, had in an article suggested that the Igbo of southeast Nigeria – the third largest ethnic group in the country – was not likely to produce the country's president in 2011 because the Northern section could not possibly give consideration to the aspiration of the Igbo.[7] Flowing from Abati's assertion is a notion, popular among Nigerians, about certain ethnic groups and individuals being privileged with power. An idea of spatialisation of power inherent in ethno-regional competition for political positions thus gives identity to power and represents decisions on who wields power as intricately bound with a notion of the socio-economy of power.

It is within the above frame that I attempted to make sense of the truncated aspiration of Taiwo. First, I had assumed that he indicated interest in the position of youth leader because he thought himself to be a member of the family quarter to which the position was zoned. It was the first time that he would attempt to access a resource, presumably the lineage's, but unfortunately, he was turned down. Taiwo's failure to attain the position of youth leader is explained by many informants in terms of the centrality of legitimacy to resource allocation. From the different accounts collected of the story, the core issue boils down to a segmentation of the lineage system in a way that suggests a scale of rights and privileges of members. Generally, among the Yoruba, though every member of a lineage is entitled to its patrimony, there seems to be a kind of kinship ranking, which imposes order on aspirations of individuals. On a matter of who among the relations of a deceased should inherit his widows, there is a hierarchy of kin upon which eligibility is derived. In following this line of thought, an informant, Abiodun, has held that while Taiwo might have been prevailed upon not to contest the election for the position of youth leader, his membership of the lineage was never disputed *per se*. According to Abiodun, it was his eligibility for the position he aspired to that was contested. 'The underwear is closer to the bums than the trouser,' he said. Initially, I did not understand this perspective. But then it appeared to me that there is a strong dichotomy between attaining lineage membership and employing membership to access communal resources. Perhaps, this was what Yinusa meant when he said posthumous offspring must know their boundary. After all, legitimacy is not just about relatedness; it is a category.

Generally, Ilupeju people did not pretend that they can influence the course of every political position in the state and in the country at large. But they speak of 'small offices' that are meant to be occupied by indigenes of the community. The small offices, I guess, refer to elective positions such as councillor in the local council, chairman of the local council, and perhaps member of the state legislative assembly. As one informant told me, the rotational order adopted by the community to ensure equity in the distribution of political offices among the constituent wards also takes into cognisance the traditional lineage quarters. 'When an office is zoned to a ward, we already have an idea of the lineage that would present candidates,' said Abiodun. Most of my informants explained that a political position zoned to a lineage can only be occupied by a member of the lineage and that it is rare for an 'outsider' to compete for the same position. Abiodun, for instance, explained that whereas matrilineal kin may be integrated into the extended family system, lineage membership for the purpose of electoral competition is solely reduced to descendants along the male line.

Abiodun also spoke about the implication of conceding a position meant for a member of the quarter to someone whose circumstance of identity is known to the whole community.

> Things are now happening so fast in the modern world. Certain things that we never believed could happen in our lifetime are happening before our very eyes. Who knows whether all of a sudden, this young man we are now talking about will trace his step back to the quarter of his biological father? In case that happens, the quarter he presently identifies with would have lost their chance to another quarter.

As in most cases of political competition in Nigeria, the local election into the position of youth leader had all the trappings of identity politics. Political offices are zoned to specific identity groups and only members of such groups are considered eligible to present themselves for elections. But the major concern here seems to be less of identity authenticity and more of the transposability of Taiwo's identity. There is the fear of defection of identity upsetting the local dynamics of power. And considering that Taiwo's immediate family members never had a problem accepting him, I also suggest that the contestation built around his lineage membership connects to the aspect of prestige that is conferred on an identity group when one of the members occupies a position of authority. The inappropriateness of Taiwo's candidature can therefore be thought to derive from the untoward consequences of power being exercised by an 'outsider' on behalf of an entire lineage. For Abiodun, the thought is reprehensible, particularly since qualified individuals were never in short supply in the lineage.

Among the Yoruba, the idea that only specific individuals or lineages can aspire to certain positions suggests a conflation of power, space and identity. In common names like Adeniran, Ojediran or Ogundele, among others, the Yoruba contextualise family patrimony and delineate the space of resource appropriation – be it power or any other capital. 'Whenever the name of a brave man is invoked, it is always done with the territory,' one of my informants had said. In other words, the essence of power may not be located outside of identity. Basically, what the identity of power does is to frame certain rationality upon which capability for specific actions is defined. For instance, although both a king and a priest embody power in their own right, they are not capable of the same actions. Consequently, a member of priest lineage may not aspire to the position of a king and vice versa. Abiodun sees lineage identity as clearly embedded in the position which Taiwo sought, and since he thought Taiwo lacking the requisite identity, his exclusion from power was justified. The implication here is that a lineage will only invoke eligibility of its members to the extent that a supposed family patrimony is seen as not only personifying its identity but also imbued with power. Outside of this, every 'member' is considered as having equal rights to the resources of the lineage. Tellingly enough, Abiodun, in the entire duration of our conversation, failed to mention a particular instance of family patrimony in which a member such as Taiwo has unrestricted access to lineage resources. Since political power is also a strong factor of resource distribution in Nigeria, it is only reasonable that the identity of the wielder be put into focus. Identity itself becomes a resource for exploiting and exercising power.

Another informant, simply called Coach, described the notion of entitlement to family patrimony as driven not entirely by legitimacy of individuals but also by the economic power which an individual can muster. He described an experience of how a family patrimony was once appropriated:

> There are people in this community who have taken the titles of families which they are only connected to through the female lines just because they are rich. I was young then, but I remember that one of the prominent sons of this town had this problem when he wanted to take a family title. There was a lot of noise about him being from the female line. But the most important thing is that he finally took the title. The other contestants complained then that he spent a lot of money and offered a number of expensive gifts to induce the elders who had the last say on who got nominated.

His words particularly challenge the notion of conceptual differences I had thought existed between paternal and maternal kin relations, at least in the area of inheritance rights. The reality that Coach describes reflects the duplicitous sanctity constructed around lineage membership. As he said, 'Even the descendants of slaves now take the title of the lineage once they have the money to bribe their way through.' It therefore appears that posthumous offspring who have by dint of hard work attained high social and economic status may not be subject to discrimination as I had earlier thought, and may have access to lineage titles just like any other members of the family. The inconsequentiality of legitimacy so implied seems not to be as simple as that, though. I was told that it was not unusual for stiff opposition to emerge when a proposal to confer the title of the lineage on an individual with questionable paternity occurred, especially one whose genitor was not of patrilineal kin. Some informants hinted that opposition, in many cases, subdued by aggrieved groups, more often than not proceeded to the law courts to seek nullification of what they considered to be an inappropriate family decision.

By accepting to withdraw from a political contest due to a challenge to his paternity, Taiwo indeed committed himself to the informal process of adjudication. He was also compelled to agree to the reality of his abridged identity. Of course, such mediation processes yet abound in contemporary African societies and are popularly referenced. There is no doubt that he was coerced to withdraw from the political contest by people who manifested power based on the position they occupied in the lineage and by reason of knowledge they had of Taiwo's paternity. Thus, the question of his identity literally disempowered him, removing the very locus of his aspiration, which was membership of a quarter to which a position had been zoned. Withdrawal from the contest also symbolises the encumbrance of a troublesome identity and a creative management strategy. As it is, any posthumous offspring in that position would be willing to salvage whatever remained of his or her personhood by drawing back from the public space rather than fighting to right a supposed wrong. Apart from the predictable consequences of struggling against the lineage, any effort to openly contest legitimacy and inheritance rights is bound to remove the lid from the identity of a posthumous offspring. This can in the long run hurt them the more and have a debilitating effect on their private lives.

Just like Taiwo suggests concerning his botched political ambition in the preceding chapter, it serves the interest of individuals who are into one form of contest or another with posthumous offspring to challenge the identity of the latter and render them ineligible to access a lineage resource. Although it is the lineage sentiment that is invoked, the end has always been to help an opponent gain advantage. In other words, emphasis on identity is often made to streamline the space of political competition so as to bring about a desired outcome. For Taiwo's opponent, bringing to the fore the birth circumstance of his rival narrows the space of contest and enables him to rally primordial support behind his aspiration, which he has cloaked in family patrimony. More importantly, it also helps him to have Taiwo disqualify himself from the race. In addition, bearing in mind his soaring popularity, questioning the basic parameters of his participation is a way to deflate him psychologically and distract from the real issue of a political contest. This looks like a re-enactment of identity politics at the micro level, except for the difference that can be found in the false sense of integration that the victim (Taiwo) might be thought to have lived with since his birth. As noted earlier in this chapter, in Taiwo's political exclusion, there is the case of cultural tradition sitting back and watching as one of its very essences stumbles from the effect of a new political economy.

While cultural advocates are bound to condemn Taiwo's political exclusion as insensitive, the point that every strategy is considered fair in the competition for power echoes from the comments of my informants. Many of them who are conversant with the story did not feel too sorry for him, including Coach, a local politician, who represents the struggle for power as lacking in moral basis. Making a quote that appears to have been taken from George Orwell's *Animal Farm*, he said, 'Politics is a case of no sentimentality.' He posited that the assurance of wealth which political positions now constitute was far stronger than the respect people could show for a dying cultural practice. Many of my informants expressed a similar view and situated the popular knowledge of politics as dirty within this context. A Machiavellian orientation written all over most views speaks to the individualised mind-set that tends to be the dominant feature of postmodern Africa. In the same vein, promotion of the market system as cultural paradigm takes every other engagement into the economic realm of competitive exchanges where personal interests rather than equity inform individual decisions. For Coach and many others, posthumous offspring identity is an albatross for the bearers and will forever disadvantage them as long as political contests are waged on the altars of identity. And among the younger generation, the identity of posthumous offspring is abnormal basically because they think it cannot be rationalised, at least not within the cultural milieu that has nurtured them. A few understood that it was a traditional cultural practice in the precolonial era, but wondered why people would subject themselves to embarrassment that was ordinarily avoidable. They expressed views which suggested that posthumous offspring have a choice to make between acknowledging their biological fathers and living permanently a life of contradiction.

Whereas political aspirations could lead to the identity of posthumous offspring being contested, their participation in economic processes is less scrutinised, especially when lineage identity is not required to access economic opportunities. Generally, my informants seemed to believe that individuals with questionable identity have always managed to achieve great wealth and success in the economic sphere. Explanations are usually couched in the mythical belief about wealth being attracted to people of low social standing in a community. As one of my informants wanted me to believe, 'Slaves and illegitimate children inexplicably achieve wealth and fortune at the expense of the supposedly freeborn'. While observations about the economic success of individuals with an abridged identity may be based on experience, I think justification may be found outside of a mythical concoction. I assume it is quite rational for such individuals to pursue more rigorously higher career aspirations to counter the burden of their birth circumstances. Moreover, they could be less weighed down by kinship obligations due to their relative disconnect from majority members of the lineage. This reality could have dawned on Taiwo who seems to have opted for a different route to achieving self-authentication. The last time I saw him, he had enrolled in a higher degree programme at one of the first-generation Nigerian universities.

Posthumous paternity: Where the church stands

The church is where most marriages are contracted in southwest Nigeria. This may be due to the fact that the popular notion of statute marriage includes solemnisation by a clergy. In performing this role, different churches in Nigeria have come up with specific regulations which cover aspects of spousal selection, abstinence from pre-marital sex and the medical status of would-be spouses. I had all of this in mind when I stopped over at the Methodist Church of Nigeria in Ilupeju to capture the church's perspective of posthumous paternity.

The Presbyter of the church, the Very Reverend Adetola Okuwobi, appeared to be in his early fifties and I was in doubt about the extent of his knowledge of posthumous paternity. The man had superintended over several Methodist parishes before his itinerary ministry to Ilupeju. I met him when the church was preparing for the annual youth anniversary. In my estimation, he exuded the aura of a reformist and a populist together, especially in his lively engagements with the youthful members of his parish.

Okuwobi, in all the years of his service in the community, had not presided over a solemnisation of holy matrimony involving a posthumous offspring, but had directly observed such events at venues outside his own church. He spoke of the culture shock he experienced in respect of the practice of posthumous paternity and his impression of women that are at the centre of it. For him, 'death marks the end of a man, and a child can only belong to whoever is responsible for the pregnancy'. Of course, it is not difficult to find explanation for his orientation and the paternity ideology espoused. Christian clergies are known to be the earliest propagators of Western epistemology, which then was couched in salvation theology.

Chapter 3

The Very Reverend would not tolerate what he termed a perverse culture but, in equal vein, considered the family interest as paramount in whatever decision the church reached on matters of ceremony. According to him, the local people were very influential in many African churches, and their opinion counted on doctrinal matters. This for me was very significant, as it touches on the subject of cultural resilience. From his comments, he tended to be more pained by the consequences of an unconventional paternity for offspring, most especially because he believed children are innocently socialised into whatever identity they bear. He spoke about the biblical thrust of posthumous paternity, and narrated how Onan, one of the sons of Judah, engaged in *coitus interruptus* each time he had sexual intercourse with his brother's widow to avoid raising a child in the name of his deceased brother. I was particularly fascinated by the story, which I think, perhaps, portrays the universalism of the levirate system as a practice meant to ensure perpetuation of the lineage of a deceased man. As I expected, the Reverend affirmed that the practice had been invalidated by the New Testament doctrines, which he then suggested offer salvation in a manner different from the Old Testament's.

Okuwobi also knew about the children that were 'born from the hands' of men other than their mothers' legitimate husbands. He regarded them as children 'born out of adultery' and could not explain how their mothers' husbands came about accepting paternity. His bewilderment was just as obvious when he said, 'Up till now I still don't know what is going on, especially in the area of marriage.' The community, he suggested, was given to sexual permissiveness, and, mothers, for him, were to be blamed for a practice he said was unacceptable both in human and spiritual estimations. In referring to children born from the hands of men other than the mothers' husbands as bastards, the clergy leaves little room for debating the paternity ideology of the people. This terse inference was nonetheless emotive, as it suggests ethical values as framed solely in terms of Okuwobi's Christian faith. I did not attempt to contest any of his claims with him.

The views expressed by the Reverend conform to the pattern expected of a Christian clergy on matters of popular endogenous practices. Although the earliest African churches appeared initially to be tolerant of some of these practices, a recent doctrinal adjustment in the direction of Pentecostalism has made denominations such as the Anglicans and the Methodists maintain tougher stances on endogenous cultural practices. Hence, it is not possible for Okuwobi or any other clergy to regard posthumous paternity or the children born from the hands of other men differently. But I like the story of Onan, especially the part where the Reverend said that God killed Onan because he was not just going to perform a culturally sanctioned obligation. For, as it can be appropriately inferred, even the biblical version of posthumous paternity contains an element of a transcendental being enforcing a breach of ethical conduct. This is very similar to cultural practice of posthumous paternity, which basis is to be found in ideas of mutuality and connectedness of both the natural and the supernatural. I did not attempt to point out this parallel to Okuwobi or any other informant, but from that moment became more attentive to the manner in which endogenous epistemologies are constructed in the conversations held with local people.

Notes

1. I learned it was possible for a very senior son to inherit the wife of his deceased father, excluding his own biological mother.
2. I use the term 'direct siblings' here to denote children born by Rhoda's mother since the other children of Aduke are also considered as Rhoda's siblings.
3. These are categories I have defined. They do not constitute an exhaustive definition of power among the Yoruba.
4. Comprehensive treatment of the Aladura movement is contained in J. D. Y. Peel, *Aladura: A Religious Movement among the Yoruba* (Oxford: Oxford University Press, 1969).
5. Commentaries on the Osu caste system can be found in Ezeanya, S. N., 1968. The Osu (cult-slave) system in Igboland. *Journal of Religion in Africa*, 1, 35–45.
6. Few of those who held this view also did not believe that the practice of posthumous paternity has contemporary existence.
7. Reuben Abati, 'South-South and the Presidency', *The Guardian*, Friday, May 26, 2006.

4

Endogenous values, spatial delineation and cultural authenticity

There is a path to authenticity that tends toward spatiality. In Nigeria, the act of a male prostrating to greet an elder is an authentic expression of respect among the Yoruba, while the *edikang ikong* cuisine is associated with the Efik.[1] In both cases there is an understanding of cultural tradition as occurring purely within spatial specificity. But the problem with cultural authenticity is that it is not fixed and, in the case of African cultures, has been rendered problematic by colonial incorporation. How then can authenticity be denoted amidst the wide range of cultural materials adopted from the West and concomitant demonization of endogenous cultural values due to colonial experience? Can Africans yet recognise that which is actually 'theirs' any longer? How does 'epistemicide' provoke a denial of authenticity for endogenous cultural values among Africans?

In seeking answers to the above questions, it is necessary that we first consider the notion of cultural authenticity. Although it seems mostly applied in relation to cultural artefacts and other forms of cultural expressions, authenticity, no doubt, connects with values and other ideational components of culture. Authenticity, especially the popular usage, pertains to realness, originality and profundity. But authenticity can also read as antiquity. A cultural practice is deemed authentic because it has a timeless dimension. Primordialism, which is implicated, engenders appropriation and conversion of popular practices into identity markers of a sort. At the same time, authenticity may have to do with exclusiveness – something interpreted in the realm of 'others do or do not have it'. This other facet engages with instances of inter-group competitions, wherein exotic cultural objects are rendered useful tools for claim-making and as evidence of high culture. In every instance, however, authenticity is grounded in the assumption of an ideal and an understanding that cultural practices are constituted as systems of meanings (Geertz 1973, 1983). The authentic is in high demand, consumed, preserved and projected as symbol of cultural integrity except when it has assumed new meanings over time.

Sometimes, the borderline between the authentic and inauthentic is simply blurred. This can happen when certain cultural artefacts and values exist clearly outside the spatial domain in which they are thought to be authentic. It may not be that they are foreign, as a particular usage of authentic will suggest. Rather, the authenticity of such objects or values is usually lost to a process of de-legitimation, especially in the case when essence or pertinence has been subjected to external validity. Hence, within the interplay of traditionalism and contested modernism, the authentic is constantly being unauthenticated, even as people quickly lose memory of their initial ownership of or an existing connection with cultural objects and values. The scale might differ from one cultural site to another, depending on the dynamics of colonial incorporation that had played out.

'This cannot be a Yoruba practice' and other like responses were the only responses I received from a number of colleagues at the university to whom I related the story of the 'unusual' Ilupeju wedding ceremony I had attended, which formed the basis of my research. Some of them questioned the Yoruba identity of the Ilupeju-Ekiti people and others even went on to suggest names of contiguous ethnic groups from which they thought the practice of posthumous paternity had filtered into Ilupeju-Ekiti, a Yoruba speaking community. There are sufficient grounds to both agree and disagree with them. Questions abound about the homogeneity of the Yoruba identity or what exactly qualifies as Yoruba culture. Is cultural authenticity among the Yoruba collectively produced across the many Yoruba subgroups or could it be that there are multiple authenticities based on the different subgroups along which the Yoruba are classified? In this chapter, I consider posthumous paternity, especially the doubts built around it, as a terrain for interrogating the subject of cultural authenticity among the Yoruba.

In pre-colonial times, Yoruba subgroups such as the Ekiti, Akure, Owo, Akoko, Ondo, Ikale and Ilaje maintained close affiliation with neighbouring Benin, and are thought to have had much of their cultural tradition hybridised due to constant interactions across the borders.[2] Popular and scholarly discourse sometimes represents them as less Yoruba due to the distinctiveness of their dialects and some aspects of their social organisation that distract from what is considered the Yoruba cultural mainstream.[3] It is in this respect that I found in the 'frontier' perspective a useful tool for explaining the contestations that form around posthumous paternity as an authentic cultural tradition of the Yoruba. Such interest flows from the suggestion of frontier as 'a force for culture-historical continuity and conservatism' (Kopytoff 1987, 3). My intention here is not to suggest the Ekiti as a group formed out of the interaction between the Yoruba metropole and the Benin. Rather, with the frontier perspective, I aim to explain cultural perpetuation as produced from the endless possibilities which a frontier space offers. Hence, the notion of frontier I attempt is of crossroads where cultural articles, values, and ideas intermingle to project not just the embeddedness of endogenous cultural repertoires but also an idea of cultural uniformity, which Igor Kopytoff aptly captures as 'similarities through convergence' (1987, 15). Moreover, frontier populations, I suggest, are likely to be agents of cultural preservation due to their occurrence away from the metropoles, which are not known to be given to cultural conservatism.

The core premise of this chapter is that posthumous paternity attests to a level of cultural integration in African societies prior to colonial intrusion into the cultural landscape. The differences in modes of widows' second marriage options practised across ethnic borders, I argue, is a reflection of the way modernity is negotiated across societies. Inability to locate initial harmony in the African reality accounts for the waves of ethno-nationalism that have resulted in violence and problems of governance all over the continent. It all seems that the definition of Yoruba culture and identity, currently dominant, is structured by pre-colonial and colonial relations of power among the several Yoruba subgroups. The pre-eminence accorded one of the subgroups reflects in the nature of the Yoruba kinship system, explicated in the colonial literature, especially the works of Lloyd (1955) and Schwab (1958). This chapter, in a way, aims to update the literature on the Yoruba creative kinship practices based on the little but significant evidence from Ilupeju-Ekiti. It starts by showing how posthumous paternity highlights the problems that are entailed in defining what constitutes the culturally authentic among the Yoruba. Then it closely examines the Ekiti area as a frontier zone, and finally the changing notion of illegitimacy in the Yoruba culture.

Posthumous paternity and Yoruba cultural authenticity

It is instructive that almost all Yoruba subgroups trace their origin to a mythical centre, Ile-Ife, which in the local cosmology is the site of creation. Apart from the traditions of common origin, Yoruba subgroups are also united in their language, and, to a certain extent, in similar symbols and customs surrounding political and mystical authority. But that is perhaps where the narratives of unity end. Interestingly, Yoruba subgroups did not at any period in history form themselves into a single political unit, and scholars have long argued that an ethnic group consciousness was indeed absent among the various subgroups as they all, in the pre-colonial era, preferred their distinctive identities (Law 1991). Quite often, the idea of ethnic Yoruba being a colonial creation has been advanced to explain a few but yet notable differences in the cultural traditions of the subgroups. The name, Yoruba, is said to have become a collective identity only in the second half of the 19th century after the colonial authority had extended it to all the linguistic and cultural groupings that claim common origin from Ile-Ife (Bascom 1969). Prior to that time, Yoruba was strictly applied to the Oyo subgroup.

While the Yoruba had in the postcolonial period formed a homogenous ethnic group, variations nevertheless occur in the local customs of subgroups. These variations I argue are produced from the differentiated encounters of the subgroups and may not necessarily suggest an absence of shared cultural traditions. For instance, whereas the northwestern Yoruba had throughout the pre-colonial period engaged in much interaction with the Nupe ethnic group, the eastern Yoruba were more involved in relationships with the Benin. Each of these subgroups appears to have an abundance of cultural forms it shares with ethnic groups it has come into contact with. The question then arises, can Yoruba cultural authenticity be produced from the numerous inter-cultural encounters which the subgroups had?

I have identified three spaces of cultural authenticity relevant to the discussion in this chapter. The first is the political; the second is both philosophical and ideological, while the third is mostly connected to customary practices. Available oral traditions of the Yoruba link the authentic political culture of the people to Ile-Ife. Starting from the early 20th century and evidenced in numerous colonial intelligence reports it became the norm for every subgroup to validate its Yoruba origin and chieftaincy institution with a narrative of migration from Ile-Ife. The narratives establishing connection also commonly include claims to an authentic crown thought to belong to Oduduwa, the mythical progenitor of the Yoruba. Although there are a few dissenters to this form of political authenticity, it has persisted and has been made more auspicious by the perceived gains of ethnic consciousness in post-independence Nigerian politics.[4]

The second domain of authenticity is also less contentious. All subgroups seem to subscribe to a philosophy of *Omoluabi*. An endogenous form of thought, *Omoluabi* is regarded as the definition of an 'ideal being', a standard of morality which entails good character demonstrated in speech, manner, hard work, bravery and truthfulness, among other virtues that the Yoruba regard as the basis of their distinctiveness. The philosophy of *Omoluabi* makes the Yoruba, and the consciousness is not only shared by all subgroups but overtly promoted as a factor of a cultural sophistication, which the Yoruba people often suggest has placed them above other ethnic groups in Nigeria.

At the level of customs, there appears to be less uniformity, at least in the contemporary age. While it is possible that basic practices relating to kinship, marriage and rituals, among others, flow from one epistemological source, their modes of expression have differed from one subgroup to another in recent years.

For instance, the practice of the Ilaje subgroup in which the corpse of a married woman is returned to her patrilineal quarters for burial differs from what occurs in many other subgroups where such a corpse is buried in the husband's family quarters. Even when some of the practices might actually have been examples of cultural resilience, their absence in the invented Yoruba culture centres has caused such values and beliefs to be viewed as being of extraneous cultures and markers of undesirable distinctiveness for marginal subgroups. Interestingly, most evidence of internal diversity is downplayed in existing ethnographic accounts, especially those published in the colonial and early post-independence eras, as they tend to define the Yoruba in terms of the basic cultural elements of the Oyo subgroup. This, of course, is understandable following the political ascendancy of the Oyo during the century preceding Western colonialism.

Representing the ideal in Yoruba culture, or any culture for that matter, may therefore be as problematic as determining which of the numerous dialects of the Yoruba language is authentic. It may not be too important here that a particular subgroup's dialect is currently the standard form of the language. Since other subgroups' dialects have continued to survive and enjoy extensive use by members, every suggestion of authenticity made with regards to the standard dialect cannot be absolute. Despite the element of power that is constantly being deployed into the definition of the ideal, it has never been easy inserting extraneous cultural practices into the collective consciousness of a people or eliminating from a social context a custom that has rightly or unjustifiably assumed the status of an ideal. In other words, cultural authenticity may not dwell in the endorsement or widespread integrity of a cultural practice. For instance, the fact that the Oyo dialect is the most widely spoken form of Yoruba does not make it authentic or render the Ondo dialect with limited speakers less authentic. This is, in essence, the summary of my discussion in the remainder of this chapter about the status of posthumous paternity as an authentic cultural tradition of the Yoruba.

What does it mean when people say that posthumous paternity was hardly an authentic Yoruba culture? Two things can be deduced from such an assertion, either that the practice was imported, or that the practitioners were not to be regarded as Yoruba. Whichever is meant, one is likely to be confronted with a notion of authenticity as connected to differences — the 'little differences' that exist among the Yoruba subgroups. Interestingly, comments about posthumous paternity not being an authentic Yoruba cultural tradition were made by people who belong to what is generally regarded as central Yorubaland. In the years of doing fieldwork among different eastern Yoruba subgroups, I have come to an understanding that internal differentiation of the Yoruba identity has been expressed in taxonomic terms such as *ara ilu oke* and *ko'nlolo*, among other categories that sometimes carry derogatory meanings. These sobriquets also embed ascription of behavioural traits such as inflexibility, treachery, craftiness and stinginess to specific subgroups. In a circumstance like this, the idea of cultural authenticity is indeed limited by the inclination of the numerous Yoruba groups to see themselves as one people.

But an assumption of the culturally authentic as primordial knowledge or the culturally familiar poses a different but important question about the status of endogenous practices that have over the years been victims of colonial epistemicide. Are they to be considered inauthentic on the strength of remoteness from the contemporary reality? From the manner in which some of my informants spoke of the endogenous cultural past as a period of ignorance, authenticity seems to be experiential, by which I mean those practices that make sense within a particular milieu. In other words, there may not be absolute authenticity, but a construct continuously negotiated across time and space.

The suggestion of posthumous paternity being hardly Yoruba reflects clannish divisions of the Yoruba as much as it is illustrative of the dominant attitude of metropole subgroups toward cultural identities of ethnic periphery. More often than not, claims of sophistication by cultural metropoles, especially the Oyo subgroup, are expressed in terms of denunciation of particular endogenous values and depiction of communities where such values have survived as backward. This follows a regular pattern in which chauvinistic remarks are passed on other ethnic groups' cultural apparatuses, especially those that are considered weird and disagreeable. The sentiment of my informants would also take for granted the presence of a benchmark upon which a practice would qualify as of Yoruba or otherwise. For this category of people, cultural authenticity is basically coloured by a sense of legitimacy, and a warped form of legitimacy for that matter, which probably sees the obscene in the continued practice of posthumous paternity. In other words, a practice viewed as culturally obscene can never be an authentic aspect of Yoruba culture, regardless of how a notion of cultural obscenity itself is historically shaped and cultivated. Moreover, there is also a way in which a hint is offered about the level of knowledge produced and disseminated of endogenous epistemology. What I find particularly remarkable in this case is that many of the people that question the authenticity of posthumous paternity as an aspect of Yoruba culture are also quick to ascribe the culture to neighbouring ethnic groups. This makes cultural authenticity look like a strong factor for delineating ethnic borders. From all of this, it would seem feasible to suggest that perhaps popular endogenous epistemologies pre-empted the colonial partitioning of the African landscape and that this thus occurred along different divides. We know this is not so.

Sometimes the prevailing local attitude toward posthumous paternity has suggested the practice as a cultural anathema. This happens to be the case with the secrecy that is built around the identity of living posthumous offspring. But a different picture is also offered whenever people describe posthumous paternity as belonging to the era 'when eyes weren't yet opened' or 'when eyes were yet dark'. The fact here is that there is the space of authenticity shifting and adjustments often being made on the basis of cultural flows (Lu & Fine 1995). Authenticity as it pertains to posthumous paternity then appears to have less to do with the internal validity of a culture and perhaps more to do with a legitimacy sought under the currently dominant Western epistemology.

But does posthumous paternity really convey an 'accurate' picture of endogenous Yoruba culture? What values are at its heart and how do such values connect to the everydayness of the people? To what extent would internal differentiation of the Yoruba undermine an effort to define what is true or otherwise about the Yoruba culture? These questions are germane, even when a particular notion of authenticity treats the concept as entirely lacking in objectivity and thus open to negotiation and contestations (Lu & Fine 1995; Peterson 2005). Rather than taking this approach, which offers an exit route away from the debate provoked by the challenge to the Yorubaness of posthumous paternity, I found it useful to outline the very substance of the arguments; that is, establishing the practice as entrenched in an endogenous epistemology, which speaks to spatial interconnection, in addition to manifesting endless cultural possibilities.

Informants' stories about widows' remarriage practices, which I initially thought were not relevant to my research, offer some insights that show connections to the pluralistic assemblage nature of the Yoruba universe. According to one interpretation of '*opo sisu*', which an informant offered, a widow is retained within the lineage of the deceased husband because 'the dead has the capacity to look back to evaluate how the lineage treats his earthly possessions – wife and children'. The dead, I was told, was never to stay away from his family, although there were exceptional cases when he might be seen as remote or totally disconnected, especially where the children suffer innumerable mishaps. Many of my informants situate the continued procreation of a deceased husband within this boundlessness. They tend to say that the door of physical and bodily existence, which death closes, is subsequently opened in the form of infiniteness, which death equally confers. This perspective differs completely from the levirate explanation, which, to all intents and purposes, constitutes a widow primarily in terms of a material acquisition, or rather explains her transfer in pure economic terms. The limit of the latter perspective is further made explicit by the fact that the widow's new 'husband' may offer little or no economic support to her and the children, as we know from one of the cases described in Chapter 2.

Another way to look at posthumous paternity in relation to Yoruba cultural apparatuses is to consider other similar Yoruba cultural beliefs such as '*akudaaya*' and '*abiku*'. Although informants' stories of widows' remarriage practices did not explicitly establish a connection with these beliefs, the current effort at affirming Yoruba authenticity of posthumous paternity may depend much on how these other beliefs are interpreted. Interestingly, there are enough mentions of them in the literature of Yoruba cultural inventories (Morton-Williams 1960; Eades 1980; Awolalu & Dopamu 2005). More than anything else, Yoruba beliefs about '*akudaaya*' and '*abiku*' inscribe not only the transitory nature of death, but also the inseparability of the Yoruba worlds of the living and the dead. Just as it has been possible to ascribe agency to the dead in respect of the two, so it would be logical to assume authenticity for posthumous paternity following the similar circumstances in which the three concepts are operationalised.

Levirate or widow inheritance

The discourse and practice of posthumous paternity in Ilupeju as I found it, is well embedded in the practice which anthropologists have described as levirate. The practice is attested to by informants and openly expressed as an elemental aspect of the people's worldview, though most times confined to the past. A number of people I spoke to, including Michael Daodu (also known as Chief Olibele), the head of kingmakers in Ilupeju, affirmed the position of the lineage heir as a surrogate for a widow's deceased husband. They also described posthumous offspring as having unlimited inheritance rights within the lineage. To further confirm the authenticity of posthumous offspring, some informants drew my attention to the fact that the same kinship terminology, *omo* (child), applies to them and other children sired by the deceased in his lifetime. In Ilupeju, there is no kinship terminology to denote whether a person is a posthumous offspring. Generally, the Yoruba employ an adjective to denote difference, as in when an illegitimate child is referred to as *omo ale*, a concept I return to later in this chapter. While this argument seems plausible, it is not without some lacuna, which can be associated with what William Schwab, in describing the Yoruba kinship terminology, aptly captures as 'a relative poverty of kin terms' (1958, 307). Moreover, *omo*, although referring to a person's child, could also mean anyone of the status of a person's child. The term is not fixed, and usages apparently reflect both the communitarian tendency of the Yoruba and the stress people place on age as an organising principle of social relationship. In other words, the absence of kinship terminology for posthumous children may not expressly amount to them having equal status with other children.

Reference to levirate is not usually made without a mention of how contemporary society has undergone changes, and the attendant implications of cultural transformation for the indigenous value system. The idea of antiquity inherent in most comments on posthumous offspring is also used to communicate the levirate as a cultural misnomer and a practice which the people have since abandoned. By and large, efforts to situate levirate in the remote past mostly reflect the burden of identity borne by present day posthumous offspring. Perhaps it is in the context of the burden that the shawl of secrecy is spread over every vestige of levirate, particularly the offspring. Interestingly, it is also within the very contestation of posthumous offsprings' identity that the practicality or continuation of levirate itself is entrenched. Some informants might have denied its contemporary reality, but those posthumous offspring whom I interviewed did not deny the circumstance of their birth. For example, the intention of Tayo who freely describes herself as '*omo oku orun*' may not be to justify her posthumous offspring identity. She nevertheless provides insight into the cultural ideology that defines her person. But she is also aware of the strangeness of her paternity and its rarity, even in the community where she lives. Hence, it is from a combination of acknowledgement of cultural change with regards to levirate and living evidence of the practice that its authenticity is articulated.

Every form of challenge to levirate as a feature of the Yoruba kinship system is strengthened by the knowledge of widow inheritance (*opo susu*) not just as a cultural tradition but as a practice that has endured to the present. The practice is known to a wide range of my informants that cut across old and young generations, even though a few manage to confuse it with levirate. Generally, widow inheritance is justified upon the notion of a widow as her deceased husband's property, although informants maintained a different stance on the paternity of offspring, which they all agree belongs to the new husband. The logic of the paternity status, according to one of my informants, is that 'like every other property of her deceased husband, the widow is inherited by an heir who now holds title to her'. Remarkably, the idea of women as property of their husbands has been used to justify the practice of levirate, especially the continued procreation of a man posthumously. But in all of this, I somehow find the aspect of title transfer fascinating. It is almost like saying that the perpetuation of title implicated in the doctrine of bridewealth is only enforceable through an heir who subsequently exercises ownership rights. In other words, such an heir holds the paternity of children conceived and born by a widow he has inherited. Somehow, knowledge and operation of the two basic widow remarriage options in the same community necessarily create confusion as per the authenticity of either as an indigenous practice. Which of the two actually represent the Yoruba ideology of widow remarriage? How is it that the two are known and practised in Ilupeju? The implied duality means that the community operates an exceptional widow remarriage practice that is different from what obtains among other Yoruba subgroups that are known for practising only widow inheritance. In Osogbo, for instance, William Schwab reported a practice of widow inheritance where in the case of a woman being pregnant at the time of her husband's death, marriage to the heir is postponed until parturition to ensure that the paternity of the child is not obscured (1958, 305). This example simply suggests a zero tolerance for the idea of an heir helping a deceased to father more children.

There are at least three ways in which the duality of widow remarriage options among a Yoruba speaking group can be explained. The first is levirate as an alien trait that diffused in from the non-Yoruba groups with whom the Ilupeju had a history of interaction. Here, attention will easily go the direction of the Benin whose suzerainty in the pre-colonial era was reported to have covered many of the subgroups occupying the eastern borderline of Yorubaland. Evidence of influence is found in areas of political and social organisations. For example, Benin chieftaincy titles such as Ologbosere and Ojomo (Ozomo) occur in many Ekiti communities. In the same manner, coral beads and other forms of body adornments typical of the Benin are lavishly used by the Ekiti during important ceremonies. In addition, the Benin society, though never the classical example of the levirate system in Nigeria has also been associated with the practice of a widow raising children on behalf of her deceased husband (Omoera n.d.). While this does not necessarily suggest Benin as the source of Ilupeju levirate, it nonetheless creates an impression of association based on proximity. However, within this history of connection we may find it difficult to explain the recent tendency of the Ilupeju people to denounce levirate and promote widow inheritance.

'The making of the Yoruba,' to use the phrase from Peel (2000) also helps to explain the shift between levirate and widow inheritance in a Yoruba speaking community. The Yoruba were never a homogeneous ethnic group or a nation prior to the creation of Nigeria as a British colony. Rather, the different subgroups were politically independent of one another, maybe until the emergence of the Oyo subgroup as a dominant regional power in the 18th and early 19th centuries. The colonial period thus marks the beginning of propagation of Oyo values as Yoruba values, and the subordination of other subgroups' cultural apparatuses. Hence, when people talk about Yoruba culture today, it is usually accompanied by an expectation of uniformity premised on Oyo standards. Internal diversity, when acknowledged, is only expressed to the extent of deviation from Oyo. From what the people of Ilupeju said of the two practices, it is highly likely, as I am inclined to suggest, that widow inheritance is a successor of levirate. Incorporation into the Oyo culture, often described as the Yoruba mainstream, possibly allowed this Ekiti community to participate in two cultural traditions, of which the levirate is indigenous.

The third explanation, which I pursue vigorously in the remainder of this chapter, contemplates widow inheritance, wherever it is practised, as an upgrade of levirate.

However, rather than constructing the relationship between the two in evolutionary terms, as I was tempted to do initially, I argue that forces of political economy compelled the change from levirate to widow inheritance, and from widow inheritance to what I call widow autonomy. In Ilupeju, for instance, the peripheral presence of levirate and the fading practice of widow inheritance both survive even within a growing acknowledgement of widow autonomy as illustrative of modernity (*olaju*) or the 'Christian age' as an informant put it. I nonetheless suggest that change from one widow remarriage option to the other reflects the degree of complexity of local political and economic processes. In other words, levirate and widow inheritance are thought to be correlates of different production eras, with strands of each surviving in isolated contexts well beyond when change had been effected, as found in the Ilupeju example.

The political economy explanation I attempt here situates change in widow remarriage options within the context of the empowerment of different actors connected to widowhood practices. The major ones are widow, lineage heir, children conceived and born by a widow after her husband's demise, and the lineage of a widow's deceased husband. The advent of wage labour, I argue, has resulted in greater autonomy for individual agency and a freedom from control of the lineage. One way in which this freedom has been expressed is for the lineage heir to assert claim over the child he fathered. Similarly, the widow, I suggest is inclined to ascribe the paternity of her child to her present husband, as this is bound to translating into greater power for her.

Revisiting the Yoruba concept of (il)legitimacy

The Yoruba speak of the illegitimate child (*omo ale*) within the family system, but, in actual fact, it appears the notion is absent in their worldview. Ordinarily, the idea of *omo ale* speaks to a child's inferior status among other children and societal disapproval of a woman getting involved in marital infidelity. It is a concept produced independently of the ingredients of legitimacy enunciated in English common law adopted by Nigeria, and emphasises the status of children of mothers who were unmarried or involved in adulterous affairs (Coker 1966, 266). Conditions of legitimacy include the following: The existence of a valid marriage between the parents of the child (customary, Islamic or statutory law marriage); the wife being the mother of the child in question; and the presumption of the father to be the husband of the mother of the child born during the subsistence of the marriage.

Illegitimacy among the Yoruba, however, is depictive of a child's lack of connectedness with the father's lineage. Hence, defining *omo ale* could be more complex than is suggested from everyday usage. Though tied to paternity, many of my informants employ several phrases that portray illegitimacy as an expressive identity, which invariably is invoked by the bearer's inevitable misdemeanour. For example, it was a common assertion that 'the cohesion in a family only subsists till such time that the illegitimate child therein comes of age.' What this means is that there is the belief that *omo ale* is bound to embark on a journey of self-destruction upon which the 'true' status of the child will be defined. Hence, it appears that the basis of the definition is the initial doubt of paternity rather than the misconduct, which sometimes is interpreted as a mark of the blood ties a child shares with the father or other prominent member of the lineage.

There is also a sense of incompletion implicated in the identity of *omo ale*. When placed side by side with its antithesis, *omo oko* or a legitimate child, *omo ale* is devoid of a critical element of claim-making, which blood relatedness represents. For them, inclusiveness in the family is not given but based on acknowledgement of paternity, which sometimes is nothing more than goodwill. *Omo ale* also goes beyond being a biological construct and tends to encompass every form of rebellion or disloyalty a person displayed toward a cause represented as the families'. A code of legitimacy is summarised in the proverb: 'It is an illegitimate child that points at his father's house with the left hand.' In this case, illegitimacy entails a tendency to forge alliances with out-group members at the expense of kinship relations.

Evidence from across Yorubaland suggests that children commonly referred to as illegitimate enjoy similar succession and inheritance rights as their legitimate counterparts. And, unlike the Igbo of southeast Nigeria, the Yoruba consider every child a man accepts paternity for as a worthy successor. This stance on legitimacy existed prior to the enactment of Section 39(2) of the 1979 Constitution, re-enacted as Section 42(2) of the 1999 Constitution, which provides that 'No citizen of Nigeria shall be subjected to any disability or deprivation merely by reason of the circumstances of his birth.' Even the practice of a woman bearing a child from the hand of a man other than her husband is well embedded in an appropriation process validated by consanguinity and the phenomenon of bridewealth. From the foregoing, it seems the most important factor of legitimacy is the father whose acknowledgement of responsibility for conception is central not just to paternity but to the social standing of a child.

Thus, it is rare that a child can be illegitimate. From what I was told, only an unmarried woman with many lovers is likely to have the paternity of her child disputed. Apparently, she lacks domestic and cultural protection similar to an adulterous married woman. The immunity which is granted married women also applies in many other African societies, especially where payment of a woman's bridewealth constitutes a basis of legitimacy for her offspring. On the position in Lesotho, Sebastian Poulter stated:

> Traditionally a child was treated as legitimate if its mother was validly married at the time of its birth. The child then belonged in the lineage of its mother's husband since his family provided the bohali. Children born of adultery were included, unless the mother was promptly divorced by her husband. So were children conceived after the husband's death, whether in consequence of Kenelo custom or a result of an informal union. (Poulter 1977, 78)

Lloyd (1955, 241) describes an illegitimate child as belonging to the lineage of its mother, and the woman's father as responsible for performing ceremonies associated with birth. Illegitimacy in this instance is not in doubt, although it may not be made obvious in social interactions and everyday organisation of the lineage.

Notes

1. The Efik are a majority ethnic group in the southeastern part of Nigeria.
2. The oral traditions and accounts of origin of these Yoruba speaking subgroups are full of references to the Benin kingdom. The connections in the history of the Benin kingdom and Yoruba subgroups such as Ekiti, Akoko and Owo is comprehensively discussed by S. A. Akintoye in his article "The North-Eastern Yoruba Districts and the Benin Kingdom", *Journal of the Historical Society of Nigeria*, Vol. iv, No. 4, June 1969, pp. 539–553.
3. For instance, a former Governor of Ogun State, Nigeria, Chief Olusegun Osoba, was quoted to have said in an interview published in the Sunday June 19, 2011 edition of *This Day* newspaper in an article entitled, "Power and Security will determine Jonathan's fate in 2015": 'If you look at all the coasts of the South West, all those living there – the Ilajes are all Ijaws – They are descendants of Ijaws …'
4. The Awujale, paramount ruler of Ijebu-Ode, in an interview with P.M. News, published June 25, 2010 stated that the Ijebu migrated to their current location from Waddai, Sudan. However, there are other accounts that associat the Ijebu with Ile-Ife, the presumed cradle of the Yoruba.

5

Neo-repugnancy: Assisted reproduction as an obscenity

> Those who move or are moved tend to position themselves or be positioned in relation to those they meet. Who gets to move why and how determines whose version of what encounters is visible or invisible in local and global marketplaces of ideas. (Francis Nyamnjoh 2012, 130)

As a primary school pupil in the 1980s, the daily morning assemblies were characterised by songs. One of the numerous songs, which I have always remembered, represented a visit to London as an ultimate ambition that we, pupils, must strive to achieve in our lifetime. Each time we sang the song, the image of the Queen's land loomed in my heart, and I assumed every one of us then understood that only hard work would make the dream of physical contact with London come true. But as young pupils then, I remember that we also managed to find parallels between the Western ways and our own lifeworlds, which we inexplicably believed was inferior. In clichés such as 'the white man drinks tea, I drink pepper soup…it is all about drinking something hot', we constructed a notion of contentment in our own reality. Somehow, I have since developed an impression that our sentiment in this regard was highly romanticised and perhaps borne out of a perceived inability to suddenly become Western. For one thing, there existed no doubt that we all formed ourselves and our ambitions in relation to a world we considered more sophisticated than our own 'rural' communities. This is mostly about the colonial legacy in which many Africans, indoctrinated in the mould of the Orwellian sheep, will feel no pain to render 'four legs good, two legs better'.

The colonial encounter produces a singular consequence for African endogenous epistemologies – alienation and subordination. Many African values, from being regarded as barbaric to being prohibited, no doubt wore the garb of the obscene.

Chapter 5

Yet contemporary experiences show that some of the much-disparaged values have equivalents in Western modernity and modes of being. A student of mine once asked me the point of difference between the Yoruba juju incantations and the Pentecostal Christians' practice of speaking in tongues. Another asked how the Yoruba have managed to replace their own story of creation, in which Obatala poured sand from a snail shell to form dry land, with the Judeo-Christian story, wherein a supreme God pronounced the universe into existence. Of course, the similarities, in form and function of the two stories, appear striking, and are capable of inviting introspection on universalism, which is generally ascribed to Western epistemology. For instance, we may want to know the forms in which sameness and difference are produced across contrasting epistemologies. Can science and 'superstition' actually find common ground in modes of being? Questions of this nature challenge the grandiose construction around Western consciousness and its accompanying values, while also capturing the frictions and tensions that are embedded in epistemological imperialism.

In this chapter, I explain the observable intersections in the logics of posthumous paternity as realised in Ilupeju and the new practices of artificial reproduction (AR) or assisted reproductive technology (ART) – a product of Western epistemology now being reproduced on a global scale. I illustrate the interplay of colonial power in the production of Ilupeju posthumous paternity as unusual and obscene. In this respect, I examine the different arenas of parallels in posthumous paternity and assisted reproductive technology: the question of the 'naturalness' of birth, the notion of help, the idea of relationality, and more importantly, the problems of the legitimacy and rights to inheritance of offspring. Central to my concern here is how a paternity ideology treated mainly as spurious is performed within the context of the contemporary practice of assisted reproductive technology. By 'performed', I mean the theatricals of conception in which fertility doctors and their clients are involved. This has got to do with commercialisation and commoditisation of reproduction and the attendant objectivisation of women's sexuality. The yielding of a woman's reproductive assignment to an agency other than the husband, the waiting period observed to get assured of successful conception, the different observances meant to safeguard pregnancy, the predictability of multiple births, and the anxiety characterising the entire process of assisted reproduction all portray an exceptional performance in which actors who also constitute the audience enact roles that produced conception as mediated or 'unusual'. Hence, in 'performing the obscene' is the idea of Western epistemology, by its practice of assisted reproductive technology, embracing a paternity sense that operates outside conventionality in a manner similar to the Ilupeju posthumous paternity.

In 1984, a report on human fertilisation and embryology, otherwise known as the Warnock report, was published in Britain. The issue of legality of embryo research that came up with the report was widely debated and finally resolved in the British Parliament in 1990, although controversies continued to trail the adoption of reproductive technologies (Shore et al., 1992). Unfortunately, Nigeria and many other African countries were not privileged with opportunities to subject assisted reproductive technologies to public deliberation before embracing a set of practices that introduced new possibilities in conception and, by implication, a new mode of being. As at the year 2015, it remained unclear if any country in Africa had formulated a policy or legal document on assisted reproduction. This may somehow suggest the unpopular nature of ARTs. But among the variants, *in vitro* fertilisation (IVF) has proved not to be strange among Nigerians, especially those we can describe as the middle and upper classes. In 2014, for instance, the total number of children born through IVF was estimated to be 10 000, even as a facility in Lagos, the Hope Valley Fertility Clinic had as at 2012 reached a landmark of 1 000 babies delivered through IVF.[3] In fact, it appears an increasing number of Nigerians have in recent years come to full awareness that popular stories of miracle births by women in their 50s and 60s are indeed cases of assisted reproduction.[4] For couples who can afford it, the technology has brought joy to their homes and enabled the dreams of motherhood and fatherhood to be realised. But in celebrating these joys, it seems we should first emerge from the shadow of neoliberalism to ask how infertility among couples became a throbbing breach in African marriages in the first place.

A starting point is to see the practice of a widow procreating for the husband posthumously as attesting to the limitless possibilities that abound in the African world, as well as the notion of interconnections and interdependencies. Similar attributions are inherent in the practice of causing conception through means other than natural. It takes little effort for me to be convinced that the underlying logic for both is very similar, more so as I was able to identify some key conceptual issues that straddle both practices. For instance, I examine the concepts of 'help' and 'donation', in relation to both, focusing not on the contextual meanings, but rather the conversations so engendered. But more importantly, questions of naturalness, stigmatisation, parenthood, and what Rivière (1985) called 'the ideal of sexual and biological integrity' are rendered problematic in assisted reproduction in a way that suggests real or imagined complexity in the social identity of offspring of assisted conceptions. This chapter, therefore, also looks at the prospects which existing knowledge and experience of posthumous paternity offers for dealing with the sociocultural challenges that may emanate from AR or ART. As an anthropologist, my aim is also to provoke dialogue on the relativity of epistemology in such a way that meanings about endogenous African values are framed outside of Western universalism. In following this line of thought, I align myself with Anna Tsing's argument that 'Universals are indeed local knowledge in the sense that they cannot be understood without the benefit of historically specific cultural assumptions' (2005, 7). Even when endogenous African values have suffered obliteration, this approach should help reclaim an authenticity lost mostly to an unequal colonial encounter. Maybe the worlds of Ilupeju posthumous paternity and assisted reproductive technology have confirmed the idea my friends and I exuded as primary school pupils: 'The white man drinks tea, I drink pepper soup…it is all about drinking something hot.' It is all about possibilities.

I find it necessary to state that my intention regarding assisted reproduction is not to underscore the relationship of pater to genitor or of mater to genitrix as this has been adequately explored in the literature on ART (Rivière 1985). The examples of ARTs I treat in this chapter are those that have implications for the paternity and social identity of a child. These are artificial insemination and *in vitro* fertilisation.[2] Even though children of artificial reproduction techniques such as *in vitro* fertilisation are generally regarded as normal and naturally conceived babies, there are, no doubt, the social downsides, which are more or less latent at the point of conception, and perhaps at this early stage of the practice in African communities. Hence, assisted reproduction, I have argued, occurs within the subtleties of self-justification and impressionism that mark most Western ideas and ideals. Children begotten through the process are cyphers, essential to confront the two-facedness of the West on matters of Africa and its modes of thought. As it were, 'obscenity', in much the same way as civilisation, can too be universal.

The Yoruba naming system mostly reflects the birth circumstance of a child. Contexts captured include pre-conception, conception, delivery and post-delivery, among other day-to-day processes in which expectant parents are embedded. These, Funso Akínnásò has described as the home context. Information captured includes the special circumstance that pertains to the child at birth, the social, economic, political and other conditions affecting the family or lineage into which the child is born, the traditional occupation or profession of the parents or their lineage, and the religious affiliation or deity loyalty of the family (Akínnásò 1980, 279–283). But often, names may invoke some unpleasant memories or carry negative suggestions about the bearer. In one of my many interview sessions for this study, I was considering the implications of modernisation for the endogenous cultural practices in Africa, and an informant whose view on the paternity status of posthumous offspring was particularly critical told me a story, which illustrates the other side of naming – the use of a name for labelling.

A rich couple had embarked on child adoption although they also have a set of biological children, the story goes. The adoption took place when the biological children were still very young, and all the children grew up together without anything to suggest that a particular child was a product of adoption. Meanwhile, the extended family members knew about it and were critical of the child's membership of the lineage. Because the man was rich, they could not confront him or express their aversion to his adopted child. Many years later the man died and his remains were taken to the village for the burial ceremony. According to the story, during the elaborate funeral ceremony, all of the deceased's children were dressed in aso-ebi,[1] and a few of the extended family members, in low tones and in a mischievous manner were talking about a Fowobi being among the children. Fowobi literally means 'the one conceived with money' in the Yoruba language, and it is meant to be a vague reference to the financial burden that accompanies a birth, maybe due to infertility treatment (but not outside heterosexual conjugality) or complicated delivery. In this particular instance, it is descriptive of a status, which the extended family members, most of whom lived in the village, had found superfluous and unequal to that of the biological children. Fowobi, to them, maintains an awkward connection to the lineage – a link thought to be mediated by monetary exchange. The story did not make mention of confrontation or embarrassment for the adopted child as I initially thought it would end, but at the bottom of it is the stigmatisation, which comes with a birth or an identity considered to be unusual or inferior. Hence, within the hope which technology-enhanced birth offers for infertile couples, there are also embedded a number of social issues similar to the Fowobi story. While trying not to feign prophetic skill, seeing into the future and foretelling the challenges of authenticity that may await offspring of assisted reproduction, is not an impossibility.

When innovation is negotiated

Anthropologists' interests in assisted reproduction technology dates back to the 1980s with the publication of the Warnock Report on human fertilisation and embryology in Britain. The report generated questions about the structure of parenthood, the claim of a sperm donor over children produced by IVF, and the ramifications for laws concerning inheritance, succession and incest (Shore et al., 1992). Amidst other concerns, which are primarily about morality and ethics, Western scholars, mainly, focused their attention on what is generally perceived as the implications of practices for social concepts such as kinship, family and personhood. Shore et al., for instance, argued that technologies relating to artificial insemination 'challenge our most established ideas about motherhood, paternity, biological inheritance, the integrity of the family, and the "naturalness" of birth itself' (1992, 295). Others took turns to discuss the ways in which the new reproductive technologies threaten to disrupt the widely held assumptions about the nuclear family as a unit founded upon an ideal of sexual and biological integrity, as well as the tension that may arise from the encounter between ethics, regulation and governance, and local ideas of substance, exchange and connection (Rivière 1985; Simpson 2013). One interesting thing about the debates is the way in which Western epistemology constituted a conflict unto itself. Voices who rose in opposition to assisted reproduction demonstrated an uncommon attraction to orthodoxy, invoking continuity for both nature and tradition.

At least three elements inherent in the ART debates are profoundly relevant to what appears to be an anthropological analysis of culture change. First, tradition, and here I suppose Western ideals, is seen as internally valid, and branded as an essential of group identity. Thus, the possibility offered by assisted reproduction constitutes a cause for worry. Second, ART is believed to occur at the level of meaning-making, which is considered as imbued with a form of dynamism. In this case, it is anticipated that local ideas and official stances may differ. Third, the numerous public debates and institutional measures built around ART suggest the involvement of people in the process of cultural innovation. Nothing was decreed. We can contrast this participatory process with the manner in which African endogenous values were demonised and summarily dismissed by a colonising epistemology.

Obviously, the way ART has been negotiated into the empirical and social bodies of Western epistemology provoked a rethink on the process that oversaw African epistemicide. Looking back, one finds the African scenario aptly captured by what Francis Nyamnjoh considered a situation of those who have 'seen the light' being the best guides for the rest that are still in search (2012, 131). Unfortunately, Africa has adopted this interventionist approach in its search, though questions abound about the actual pursuit of the continent and whether its guide can really lead it to the path of self-discovery, which can actually sum up the essentialness of a search.

Maybe I should emphasise here that analysis of the paternity concerns in assisted reproduction technology, which I propose here, does not hint at smooth incorporation for a practice that has struggled for authentication. Rather my interest lies in the rupture generated by the practice being considered largely spurious and antithetical to the sociocultural ideals upon which the West had formulated relativised meanings about humanity. This, for me, sends the West to the very state Africa was in when its cultural essences were abrasively violated. Where it has left the West I do not know, but it can for one be said that concerns generated over assisted reproduction constitute a challenge to a notion of universalism, together with the rational-cum-empirical stances of Western epistemology. The very idea of assisted reproduction itself attests to the world of unlimited possibilities, around which the creative paternity practices of Africans are basically constructed.

I now turn to the unnaturalness of assisted reproduction, since colonial sentiments against posthumous paternity revolve around unusualness. My intention is to subject assisted reproduction technology to scrutiny through local experiences of *in vitro* fertilisation. This is necessary to put into perspective the role of power in the whole project of epistemological suppression. As will be shown in this chapter, the idea of natural justice, equity and good conscience (the premises upon which posthumous paternity and other similar values were proscribed by the colonial laws) though meant to project European standards of morality in Africa, is nonetheless rendered problematic in the advent of assisted reproduction. Here, I suggest that the control, which the West often exercises in the global production and dissemination of knowledge, has not prevented even Africans from seeing the practice of assisted reproduction as unnatural or strange.

Children made by doctors

Stories of miracle births are commonplace in Nigeria. Women in their 40s and 50s suddenly become pregnant after enduring some 20 or 30 years of childless marriages. The pregnancies, which often result in multiple births, are widely advertised as modern-day miracles. But, in recent times, these stories have become tainted by a growing awareness of IVF. Why do women who conceive through IVF ascribe their pregnancies to spiritual intervention? The answer definitely is unconnected to the dominant sentiment about 'assisted' birth. My point here is that denial seems to be cultivated from the very level of language.

In offering a pathway to understanding its very essence, the language of assisted reproduction takes the form of problem-solving. While 'assisted' and 'technology' easily suggest birth as mediated, other idioms of ART practice also ensure that being human is detached from the principle of naturalism, which unfortunately Western epistemology guarded jealously in its aversion to the African practice of ascribing paternity to dead persons. In its terminologies, such as 'donor', 'artificial insemination', 'sperms', 'eggs' and 'fertilisation' among others, assisted reproduction constructs a notion of human conception in purely biological terms.

Attempting a lexical analysis of these terms can perhaps lead us into the complex issues associated with assisted reproduction. Two key terms, 'assisted' and 'technology' are of importance here. As harmless as the two appear, interpreting them in terms of a sociocultural understanding of birth, especially in Yoruba society, brings out the embedded meanings that could be similar to the Fowobi story I related in an earlier part of this chapter. 'Assisted' when employed in relation to pregnancy or birth suggests unusualness and spuriousness. Here, it is not just about conception or birth lacking in biological ingredients or offspring being deficient in any aspect of child and behavioural development. Rather, it is about popular consciousness being driven in the direction of processual inversion, in which the common meanings of 'assist' as 'help', 'aid' or 'support' stimulate the sense of deficiency, particularly in the woman. The idea of 'assisted' here also pertains to the method of child delivery. For example, despite the length of time Western medical infrastructure has been available in Nigeria, the caesarean section still occurs as a point of stigmatisation for women. There is an abundance of sympathy for these women. I was told that women who undertake the process often feel inadequate as mothers. 'Most of us often pray to have natural births,' a female informant has said.

The other term, 'technology', introduces the human factor into the conception process, which all the while has been thought natural. For instance, situating ART operations within that which is known as the 'fertility industry' somehow reinforces a sense of commercialised production and of ensuing babies as crafts. Moreover, the ordinariness made of sperms and eggs conjures up the image of a manufacturing process in which biological substances assume the value and qualities of raw materials. Competition within the fertility industry can sometimes instigate strange claims. 'How many units in Nigeria have been around for nine years, and how many can boast of producing more than 900 babies?' an enthusiastic operator of a fertility clinic was quoted to have once asked. Logic of babies as commercial articles definitely flows from the word 'producing'. This apart, talking of 'boast', the operator represents ART babies as accomplishments of medical doctors and indeed of technology. A commodification process of sorts, implied in the practice of ART, in a way, reinforces the idea of assisted conception as Fowobi.

Then there is 'anonymity' as an underlying principle in donor conception. One of the reasons for this is to shield children born of donor conception from identity contestations. But it is one thing to keep a child away from vital facts about the self and another thing to prevent the mind of parents from wandering around the birth circumstance. The downside seems weightier in African societies considering the centrality of lineages as sources of social denomination.

The feelings that an assisted pregnancy is unnatural have been expressed in different ways by my informants. For example, one told me a story she read about a woman who claimed she was not enthusiastic about her daughter's pregnancy because it was assisted. According to the story, the woman would not tell her friends about becoming a prospective grandmother because 'she was not sure how the whole thing would turn out to be'. Such scepticism can of course form the basis of future relationship with the unborn child. Another informant described assisted reproduction as crafting of humans in manner similar to hi-tech products. This kind of conviction is furthered by the huge financial resources required for assisted conception and claims of expertise, which different fertility clinics continuously make. A few, however, are concerned about the biological connectedness of some IVF children.

The fact that donor sperms and eggs are sometimes utilised for *in vitro* fertilisation brings forth the question of paternity. 'There is the chance that a child conceived through this process may not share a genetic link with the father or even the mother', a female informant averred during one of my interviews. But it does not just end there. She suggested that an IVF child produced from donor sperm may suffer stigmatisation from the home front if the father afterward has another child from natural conception. Using her words, 'The sense of lack of biological connection with a child can make the father treat him differently.' Treating the child differently obviously means being discriminated against on account of birth circumstance. Another informant said that future stigmatisation of IVF children is imminent, as soon as the Yoruba have coined a name for the practice. The Yoruba she claimed are notorious for creating otherness through name-calling. From what is known of paternity practice in Ilupeju and possibly other Yoruba communities, any future stigmatisation of IVF or other forms of assisted reproduction children can only have been encrypted in a post-colonial culture that constructs belongingness mainly in terms of blood connectedness. Considering the dominant nature of identity politics in Nigeria, it will be rare for the question of individual authenticity not to be taken seriously. This leads us to the notion of legitimacy of children conceived through artificial insemination by a donor (AID).

A Report of a Government Commission set up in Britain in 1960 to look into issues of legality of AID, while discouraging the practice, observed that the husband of a woman who bears an AID child has no parental rights or duties in law with regard to that child. According to the Report, parental rights and responsibilities, in principle, reside with the donor, who could be made liable to pay maintenance, and who could apply to a court for access or custody (Rivière 1985, 3). While the subsequent Warnock Report endorsed AID and IVF, it however recommended that legislation be enacted to disinherit any child born through IVF who was not *in utero* at the date of its father's death (Rivière 1985, 6). Obviously, in the two reports, the Western epistemology has stayed committed to the idea of belongingness being achieved only by biological connectedness. But once these practices have been exported from the shore of the West, the answers to the questions to be asked of IVF and other forms of assisted reproduction may be more than the the Warnock Report can provide. Anthropologists have raised many of these concerns, particularly in relation to Western society where the practices have roots. When cues are taken from the views expressed by my informants, most disparate thoughts of IVF in Nigeria flow around the implications envisaged for social and biological identities of the offspring. But scholarly arguments may likely refract to the creative kinship practices of pre-colonial African societies, and whatever is thought to be the underlying logics of traditional practices.

Chapter 5

Two faces/phases of the repugnancy doctrine

I will now share my thoughts on a celebrated legal matter pertaining to the status of children born by widows in Nigeria. I have much interest in this particular case because of the principle of repugnancy, which forms the basis upon which the final verdict was reached. *Chinweze v. Masi* is a very popular case in Nigerian jurisprudence and any student of law will come across it in the Family Law course. In *Chinweze v. Masi*, the dispute revolves around the estate of one Peter Chinweze who died intestate. The widow, Elizabeth Chinweze had remained in her matrimonial home thereafter with her daughter (defendant/respondent) and only child from the marriage.

Long after the demise of her husband, Elizabeth Chinweze conceived and gave birth to other children (plaintiffs/appellants) whom she raised in her deceased husband's house (the property in dispute). Upon the death of Elizabeth Chinweze, the appellants approached the High Court in Enugu claiming themselves as beneficiaries of their mother estate against their sister (the defendant) based on the following: (i) A declaration that the house situated at No. 5 Ogui Road, Enugu, is the bona fide property of Mrs Elizabeth Chinweze (deceased) of whom the plaintiffs are beneficiaries; (ii) A declaration that the defendant is a trustee *de son tort* in respect of the estate of the said Mrs Elizabeth Chinweze (deceased); (iii) An injunction restraining the defendant, her servants or agents from any act of interference with the said property contrary to the interest of the beneficiaries and from dealing with it in any manner whatsoever as if it was her property (quoted in Ebeku 1994, 53–54).

The case passed through all the levels of adjudication in Nigeria. The trial judge ruled that the plaintiffs had no *locus standi* to institute action on the said property since they were not the children of the marriage of Peter Chinweze, the original owner of the property. The trial judge also averred that Elizabeth Chinweze while alive held the property in trust for herself and her daughter alone and when she died her interest in the property accrued to the defendant as the surviving joint tenant. The judgment of the High Court was affirmed at the Court of Appeal, prompting a final appeal being made to the Supreme Court.

On 27 January 1989, Oputa J.S.C. led other five justices of the Supreme Court to affirm the ruling of the trial court. Even though the appellants sued as beneficiaries of the estate of Elizabeth Chinweze, their mother, the judgement of the Supreme Court contained ingredients portending implications for the custom of posthumous paternity. The justices held as follows:

> A man's family normally consists of the man, his wife or wives and children born to him by such wife or wives. I have on purpose used the expression wife or wives because we have here in Nigeria two types of marriages recognised by law … whatever the system of marriage the undisputed fact is that the

appellants were born after the death of Peter Chinweze. They were therefore not his natural sons *for it is contrary to the course of nature for a dead man to produce children.* (quoted in Ebeku 1994, 55, emphasis mine)

A remarkable issue for determination in *Chinweze v. Masi* was 'Whether the Appellants who were born after the death of late Peter Chinweze by undisputed wife living in the matrimonial home was [sic] part of late Peter Chinweze family and could inherit part of the family property' (quoted in Ebeku 1994, 5). Apparently, this has to do with the continued validity of posthumous paternity as a traditional practice of the Igbo, the ethnicity of parties in the case.

When Oputa J.S.C. stated that it was contrary to the course of nature for a dead man to produce children, he certainly had in mind the repugnancy doctrine of colonial law (Ebeku 1994). The doctrine, which origin is in the medieval period and English Equity, was introduced into the Nigerian legal system with the adoption of English Law in the late 19th century. However, the most popular allusion to the repugnancy doctrine has been in respect of Lord Atkin's judgment in the case of *Eshugbaye Eleko v. Government of Nigeria* (1931) wherein the colonial judge affirmed thus: 'The court cannot itself transform a barbarous custom into a milder one. If it stands in its barbarous character it must be rejected as repugnant to natural justice, equity and good conscience.'[5] Although Lord Atkin's judgment also affirmed the role of communities in validating native customs and practices, it was the principle of repugnancy alluded to that has drawn most attention.

Much legal controversy has been generated around the doctrine. As Kaniye Ebeku writes about the repugnancy test, 'The problem involves what criterion or criteria to employ. Is it a universal idea of what is just or the standard of purely English or purely European or purely Christian morals or values' (1994, 59)? As an anthropologist, my interest does not lie wholly in the judicial interpretations of laws, as I seem to be fascinated more by Taslim Elias's view on law as a relative phenomenon (cited in Ebeku 1994, 59). From the beginning, the repugnancy doctrine connected to the civilising logic, and its target was endogenous cultural practices that were adjudged incompatible with Western values.

One can yet broaden the explanation around the repugnancy doctrine. Intolerance of endogenous values, which the doctrine promoted, is illustrative of power relations between colonisers and the colonised. Such power relations are enacted in the forms of dominance, and an uncompromising legitimation of Western values. By establishing dominance and epistemological superiority through legal contraptions such as the repugnancy doctrine, the colonial authority also ensured that Africans were not given options even in their own matters. Unfortunately, expectations of a resurgence of African endogenous epistemologies in the postcolony are often dashed by pronouncements of the kind made by Oputa J.S.C. But, does a suppression of local modes of thought automatically validate an imperialistic alternative? The pervasiveness may suggest the affirmative. Meanwhile, it is often said that when the pressure is on, many Africans continue to engage endogenous epistemology for solutions to life challenges.

Even when it was not particularly codified in a document, the repugnancy doctrine existed as a judicial clampdown on many traditional cultural practices including 'ghost marriage', 'women-to-women marriage' and a widow's second marriage, among others. The doctrine, as it applies to a widow's second marriage, for instance, questions the naturalness of posthumous paternity. Its essence is the inviolability of biological connectedness as the basis of determining a child's paternity. Constructed in this manner, the doctrine of repugnancy evidently gives no recognition to social paternity. As the doctrine will have us believe regarding the status of children a widow bears in the name of her deceased husband, it is quite unnatural to attribute paternity to a deceased who played no role in procreation. When it comes to defining what is natural, it should not be surprising that nature is seen and interpreted only through the prism of Western ideals.

This is where the question of assisted reproduction being either repugnant or not arises. By introducing ART into the repugnancy argument, I am not inclined toward pitching technology against popular endogenous cultural values, but want to show technology as capable of producing as much 'obscenity' as that attributed to endogenous cultural practices. What seems to matter, after all, are the context of evaluation and the identity of an evaluator. For instance, in processes of artificial insemination and *in vitro* fertilisation where donor semen is utilised, it is obvious that husbands do not contribute genetic substance to a pregnancy. On another level, freezing of semen and embryos creates the possibility of a woman having a child for her deceased husband posthumously. In these examples, technology has not in any way filled the gap created by lack of genetic relatedness between a father and a child. Interestingly, surrogacy, which is gradually creeping into global consciousness, has a *raison d'être* similar to the woman-to-woman marriage practised in pre-colonised Africa. Just like in the latter, the procreation role of a woman is contracted out.

In vitro fertilisation, which is our commonest example of ART, operates within a commercialisation ethos. Despite growing global awareness of it, only very few people can afford 'fertility treatment'. This lends credence to the popular suggestion that children conceived through IVF are not born but made. One of my informants said that she now suspects a case of IVF each time a woman who has not given birth for long suddenly delivers a set of twins or triplets. She also got to know that women who undergo IVF have a choice in the number of births they want. 'I think with that amount of money usually expended, it will be unreasonable for any woman to choose single birth when multiple births won't cost extra money', she told me. Multiple births, from my informant's perspective, are not just guided by market ethos but are as well de-naturalised. Twins and triplets ceased to be special births and are detached from human genetic properties. In thinking that it will be unreasonable to choose a single birth when multiple births won't cost extra money, she interprets decisions about conception as governed by the rational choice model. Then comes the question, could all of these realities be repugnant to natural justice, equity and good conscience or are they too just natural? Are they likely to produce a fictitious genealogy for the offspring?

Existing defence in support of IVF and other forms of ART has been mounted on the wings of science, objectivity, rationality and naturalism, among other attributions to which Western epistemology makes claims (Nyamnjoh 2012, 131). These are not just buzz words. Their usages go alongside other languages of civilisation and depictions of high culture. Interestingly, Western epistemology has only itself to convince concerning the moral and ethical correctness of ART and, once that is done, the rest can be cloaked in the language of science and advancement. Such arrogance is historically produced and lies at the bottom of many issues of theory, method and rationale of colonialism, which Cooper (2005) sums up as the 'colonial questions'.

The idea that pregnancy can be caused by money nullifies the age-long belief about children as special gift from a divine being. Such belief, of course, exists in most of the world's religions, including Christianity, which constitutes the moral and ethical platforms for Western epistemology. Thoughts of repugnancy, in the instance of IVF, will therefore relate to how a society responds to commercialised conceptions. Employing 'legal wallpaper to plaster over the cracks' (Rivière 1985, 4) may or may not lessen whatever negative perceptions people may have of assisted reproduction. Hence, with IVF deeply enmeshed in meanings that suggest it as an exercise in human fabrication, the idea of it being repugnant will actually be difficult to ignore. Even when the success rate is not total, there is a way in which IVF transforms conception into an industrial process wherein articles are made and delivered to those who can afford them. Moreover, the element of multiple births is sufficient to make the practice reprehensible to cultures that regard twins and triplets as special children.

Generally, if we are to understand the epistemological politics and hypocrisy behind the colonial repugnancy doctrine, we just need to move away from an assumption of the doctrine simply as a clampdown on 'barbaric' customs, to understanding it more as a way of enforcing subjectivity in the erstwhile colonies. If anything, it shows the politics in the entire process of cultural validation and offers credence to the view that with the repugnancy doctrine the British only bullied Nigerian customary law to their own standard of morality. Could this be a case of African societies, with their creative kinship practices, having gone a step ahead of the West in deciphering solutions for challenges relating to infertility and other problems associated with the family system?

The level of popularity which ARTs has attained in the West suggests that it is not regarded as culturally unacceptable as such.[6] The only explanation for this could be that it is technology driven, unlike the African idea of posthumous paternity, which the colonial legal instrument categorised as a practice based on 'fictitious genealogy'. In Nigeria, the oldest child to be born through IVF attained the age of 19 years in 2012.[7] The birth came 15 years after the world's first IVF child, Louise Brown, was born in Oldham in 1978. It is therefore understandable that the issue of public knowledge about ART children has not received much research attention in Nigeria. Even so, associations have been formed by ART mothers in Nigeria to campaign against the social stigma associated with IVF.[8] The consciousness built around the subject of stigmatisation is historically and culturally produced. It could most likely have drawn substantially from experiences with adoption and other traditional creative kinship practices, and perhaps the feeling of inadequacy, which parents of ARTs children have of themselves. The history of assisted reproduction, especially the opposition mounted against it, may also explain the readiness of parents to combat the social downsides at the very early stage of its evolution in Nigeria.

From what is known about it, there is nothing to suggest ART as culturally correct and worthy of necessary legal endorsement ahead of customary practices such as levirate. Current reality shows that disaggregated paternity has come to receive positive assessment as different possibilities from ARTs continue to bourgeon. Could it then be that societies with the levirate system were well ahead in envisaging social paternity as ideal form of paternity? Jacobs (2006), for instance, considers social parenthood as reflecting the panoply of actions which parentage entails. It may perhaps be argued that posthumous fathers are lacking in parental roles and are therefore not fit to be categorised as social parents. But this is an argument that will not go far considering what is known of the normative dimension of parenting. In many African societies, and among the Yoruba in particular, the notion of birth as being initiated by an individual and of parenting as a collective function of the community will not allow paternity to be constructed in terms of individual agency. In other words, the death of a man could not possibly terminate his parenting role, which he, for one, never once performed solely. The Yoruba idea of *babá kú, babá kù* correlates with the immortality of fatherhood and the assurance of continued social and economic support for children upon the demise of their father.

An interesting feature of the Warnock Committee is that it recognises that people are bound to find some of its recommendations morally objectionable. Hence it makes no pretence about the findings not conforming to a universal standard of morality by which ARTs can be adjudged as 'good, just and fair', in other words, not repugnant to natural justice, equity and good conscience. Rather, it provides for individual choices in arriving at decisions on what Simpson (2013) terms as reproductive desires. This is quite understandable, because having its cultural roots in English society and in science, ARTs can hardly be completely reprehensible. No doubt, there were strong oppositions and legal restrictions to certain aspects of ARTs at the very beginning. But most of these have been downplayed in the Human Fertilisation and Embryology Act (Amendment) of 2008. For example, the requirement to consider a child's need for a father was replaced with a requirement to consider the child's need for supportive parenting. This amendment creates the possibility for gay couples to bear children that have a genetic link to them.

With the repugnancy doctrine as it pertains to posthumous paternity, I think the colonial law was uncomfortable with the idea of a genitor being separated from the pater. But this is exactly what obtains in the case of some examples of assisted reproduction. One of my informants asked:

> If a child that is born from an adulterous relationship can be discriminated against as is usually the case, what do you think will happen in the case of a child discovered to be born from an anonymous donor sperm?

My informant affirms that the genitor of a child born from the hand of another man is often known in the community, but the same cannot be said of a child conceived from the semen of an anonymous donor. There is also a sense in which she suggests that a complete disconnectedness with the community, or consanguineous anonymity, portends bigger challenges to the social identification of ART children. In her words: 'The worst that can be done with a child born from the hands of another man is to ask him to return to the house of his biological father. But where will you ask a product of anonymous donor's semen to go?' The question is somehow pertinent considering the Yoruba belief about illegitimate children and their predisposition to digging into the social identity of people, especially at occasions of competition for resources.

Help, donation, and making women pregnant

Reading from a Nigerian IVF blog site where a gynaecologist expressed delight in helping women to get pregnant, my mind went to the cultural practice of a woman bearing a child 'from the hand' of a man other than her husband. In every instance where a woman in a subsisting marriage gives birth to a child from the hand of another man, the language of 'help' and 'donation' comes up to describe the relationship between the genitor and the woman's husband. For example, my interest in this research was originally stimulated by the language of help my primary contact in Ilupeju introduced into the practice of posthumous paternity. Mama Dele once described a man who fathered three children with the widow of her deceased father-in-law as a mere helper. By this she meant that the genitor of the children she regards as siblings of her husband has only assisted in raising more offspring for her deceased father-in-law. In my other interviews, people also talked about children being donated, most especially in reference to the phenomenon of a married woman bearing a child 'from the hand' of another man. I here try to make sense of how assisted reproduction using donor semen bears a resemblance to the practice of bearing a child 'from the hand' of another man, particularly in the aspect of both being framed in the idioms of 'help' and 'donation'.

There are of course some suggestions to be made concerning the nature of help or donation that a genitor in the traditional practice, can make. From the way informants speak, it is obvious that the idea of help or donation is solely connected to the paternity claim that a genitor loses when he causes conception in a married woman other than his wife. In such cases, the help is unsolicited and he receives neither acknowledgement nor any appreciation. The woman's husband (whether dead or alive) is deemed to have been helped not because he could not perform his conjugal role, but for the gain so made from a trespasser, so to say. It is however important we know that the language of help is not employed in a true levirate arrangement, where the levir is thought to be engaged in a cultural enactment. Hence, help in the construction of the unsolicited role of a genitor is more or less derisive and indicative of an unprofitable venture a man elects to undertake. From what I learned about it, the idea of help also applies to the act of a man having sexual affairs with a widow. Even when conception and paternity issues are not implied, the relationship is regarded as being helpful to the widow, particularly in view of the stigma the status carries in many African societies. For instance, *oko opo* is not meant to be 'husband of widow' that the term ordinarily suggests, but an insinuation of emotional obligation a man renders to a widow.

The notion of help or donation, interestingly, does not depict paternity as contested. Rather, each of the two terms is employed to validate the position of the child as a legitimate offspring of the mother's husband. In other words, labelling the genitor a helper or a donor necessarily undermines his role in conception and removes emphasis from the genetic link as the crucial factor in paternity. But, it appears this works more with widows who have chosen to remain in the compound of their deceased husbands. In other instances, a husband who for one reason or another thinks he is not responsible for his wife's pregnancy may accuse her of unfaithfulness. I was told this rarely happened in the past, when every pregnancy was assumed to belong to the husband.

In the IVF story cited earlier, the doctor spoke of the joy he had in helping to make women pregnant. This could smack of the joy of fatherhood, but it is assumed that he has in mind the intervention of assisted reproductive technology, which he leads on behalf of childless couples. Indeed, by mediating the entire process, his helper role should never be in doubt. However, 'helping to make women pregnant' goes beyond administering fertility treatment. The comment entails the almost near genitor role performed when he, the doctor, transfers the fertilised egg to a woman's uterus. It too sums up the total belief, which infertile couples, especially women, have in the doctor as the one to make them fruitful. Like the adulterous helper, the doctor has no paternity claim on a conception he has caused. But unlike him, the doctor is a solicited helper who receives monetary reward for his services. His status as a helper and one lacking in paternity claim is further enhanced by the anonymous status of the genetic substances.

The anonymous donor, as the name implies, invokes a deep sense of help and of altruism. Although the elated fertility physician in the blog story did not acknowledge the donor's contribution, perhaps due to the fact that not all cases of IVF utilises donated biological substance, I assume the donor's part in the whole arrangement to be important whenever it is required. The sperm donor as a helper is not disposed to acknowledgement and has ceded paternity *ab initio*, thereby framing conception as a biological process, which depends on social regulations for authentication. People I spoke to represent the nature of help rendered by the donor as both enduring and reassuring, considering the immunity it offers for paternity contestation. This perspective appears simplistic and dismissive of other forms of identity contestations, to which the product is susceptible. One informant mentioned inner conflict as likely to be more disturbing than the knowledge which the public has of the genitor and pater roles residing with different individuals. Cannell (1990, 673) also offers insight into the limited anonymity of anonymous donor by citing Rowland's (1985) example of Australia where sperm donors campaigned for the right to know whether or not their sperm has been used to make a child.

Generally, across the three domains discussed above, help and donation may be implied in conception but not in paternity. In essence, paternity being a cultural construction is defined mainly in terms of the position of a child in a relationship adjudged as marriage, and in the case of the Yoruba, the disposition of the putative father. With the language of help and donation appearing to set a parallel in the role of the adulterous genitor and the anonymous donor, the problem of common effect becomes pertinent. More importantly, we are confronted with that which Simpson describes as 'wider questions of relationality and exchange' (2013: S87). In reality, one is an old practice, even as the other is emerging. But then, the relevance of comparison can only be found in the challenges of paternity considered common to the two. The concern should also be about the absence of a legal framework to the practice of assisted reproduction in Nigeria and the ways in which such lacuna might resuscitate the question of repugnancy.

Mama Dele also spoke of a lady she claimed was born from the hand of her father-in-law while the latter was alive. She narrated how one of the brothers-in-law (not any of those born posthumously) had developed a love interest in the lady but was prevailed upon to look elsewhere for a wife based on the blood ties he supposedly shared with the lady. According to her, 'This lady in question has all the physical attributes that are common to all the children of my father-in-law. Even when she was not claimed everyone knew where she belongs.' It all seems that blood matters after all. But then it is not paternity that is at stake here but a possibility of incest being committed. This type of potential problem was identified with the anonymity of sperm donors, prompting the Warnock Committee to recommend that no single donor should be used more than ten times (see Rivière 1985, 6). This consciousness of blood ties means that people are familiar with certain connections, which for one reason or another are unspoken. Even when these generate gossip, there is little expectation of action being taken toward effecting changes in paternity status. Unfortunately, products of assisted reproduction may never have the benefit of social reprimand, although there are stories of resemblances provoking investigations into births from a common donor.

'ART' and the cultural construction of adultery

There was an illustration which an informant, Mama Iyabo, gave about ART and the sexuality of women. I asked her about the social implications of inseminating a woman with the semen of a donor and her thoughts indeed have semblance with the suggestion of artificial insemination by a donor as comparable to adultery. She told me of the Urhobo culture that forbids men from holding the wrist of married women or having the slightest body contact with them. Such physical contact, she said, is tantamount to committing adultery with a woman. I am aware many Nigerian cultures place restriction on bodily contact between married women and men other than their husbands. My informant described a situation where semen of a donor is required for insemination or fertilisation as technology mediated adultery. This position is not entirely new, considering that artificial insemination by a donor (AID) was likened to adultery in one of the many objections to it submitted to the Warnock Committee (Shore et al. 1992, 299). Mama Iyabo suggested that women who are desperate to have babies subscribe to ART, which involves donor semen, to satisfy the dream of having their own children. Two things can thus be inferred here. First, that the act of impregnation by donor semen is adultery. This definitely is against the popular commentary on assisted reproduction practices like IVF as a source of joy to many families. The second suggestion is that a child born through the process can only be regarded as belonging to the mother. Both propositions underscore the externality of husbands, who ordinarily are the framework of paternity, in such circumstances.

The notion of 'technology mediated adultery' may compare to the traditional practice of women whose husbands are impotent depending on extramarital affairs to raise children for their marriages, at least from the angle of the *raison d'être* for the extramarital affair. Although I am not really out to engage in a philosophical exposition on adultery, I consider the possibility of the concept being explained outside of the traditional viewpoint of sexual intercourse very interesting. The whole import will be to interpret adultery as a violation of the sacredness of a married woman's body. This is particularly in reference to restricting to the husband sexual access to the wife.

The important question is whether the sanctity of the woman's body is presumably preserved when it harbours a substance that emanates from another man from a process other than sexual intercourse. The Warnock Committee thought so when it considered AID as occurring outside the realm of adultery. The Report posits: 'AID involves no personal relationship between the mother and the donor at all, and the identity of the true father of the AID child will normally be unknown to the mother, and unascertainable by her' (Warnock 1984, 20). Interpretation like Warnock's situates adultery solely in the realm of physical interaction and ignores the ideational elements that drive most of human actions. Mama Iyabo disagreed with the Warnock interpretation and even supported her position with the Biblical account where Jesus Christ equated looking at a woman lustfully with adultery. She complicated the whole issue when she identified the anonymity involved as the most unacceptable aspect of artificial insemination. 'It is as bad as being raped', she said. This perspective sounds rather extreme but nonetheless speaks to the emotional side of ARTs and the cultural intricacies embedded in interpreting adultery. A similar sentiment was expressed by Pakistani Muslims about ARTs that involve using another man's sperm to achieve pregnancy. On their disposition, Bob Simpson said: 'To introduce the sperm of another man into a relationship would be tantamount to having had sex outside of marriage (*zina*) with the dire consequences that this would bring for the couple' (2013, S90).

In many of the informant comments, adultery is basically constructed as sexual intercourse and a pleasure-seeking behaviour that occurs well outside the intention of procreation. But most also agree that some married men and women engage in adultery to enhance their chances of procreation. Such practice, encapsulated in the language of 'testing' or 'trying' other options is said to be common with couples that are not disposed to act concertedly toward finding a solution to their infertility. The assumption that it is the other partner that is defective, I was told, drives childless husbands and wives into adulterous relationships. Some of the comments paint the picture of a reluctant wife or husband being pushed into adultery by the stigma of childlessness or barrenness. For instance, the myth of a child born from a man's adulterous relationship instigating conception in his wife is very rife. The stories, which convey the helplessness of women mostly, are similar to what I heard about couples seeking IVF treatment not minding a donor sperm or egg inasmuch as conception will be achieved. On the other hand, the idea of the couple keeping the details of IVF treatment 'between themselves' (Simpson 2013) also emerges clearly in comments informants made about children that married women bore 'from the hands' of other men. As one of them put it:

> It is not like a man rings a bell to announce to the whole community that a child his wife gives birth to belongs to another man. The knowledge is usually restricted to the man and his wife and some elderly members of the lineage. But like the Yoruba would say, any secret known to two people is no longer a secret.

In this instance, bringing lineage elders into the whole story is a way of acknowledging their role as mediator in cases where a woman is deemed to have committed adultery.

As it were, there is always the feeling of something not right with employing donor semen for fertilisation. Cannell (1990, 672) describes a donor as a potential intruder even though he might have helped in cementing a couple's relationship. In accepting the donor intervention, couples are thought to be driven by the imperativeness of experiencing the 'joy of parenthood', which is considered far more important than any reflection of the means of impregnation. Many of my female informants saw donor-enabled insemination or fertilisation as worthy mediation but would not favour having sexual intercourse with a man other than their husbands in order to achieve pregnancy. Similarly, my male informants found no connection between adultery and insemination by donor semen. Rather, they explained their dispositions to donor insemination in terms of receptiveness or otherwise of a man to the practice of adoption, which is seen as the last of the solutions to a fertility problem. 'If a man can regard an adopted child as his, there is the likelihood that he won't have problem with a woman using donor's semen to conceive', one of them said.

Notes

1. Among Nigerians aso-ebi is a uniform dress usually worn by family members and sometimes friends and well-wishers during special occasions such as wedding ceremonies and funerals.
2. Artificial insemination refers to the act of placing semen inside a woman's vagina or uterus by means other than sexual intercourse (Rivière 1985). It could be semen of the husband (AIH) or the semen of a donor (AID). On the other hand, in vitro fertilisation is when a ripe human egg is extracted from the ovary of the woman and then mixed

in vitro with semen with the hope of fertilisation. The fertilised egg (now a developing embryo) is transferred back to the uterus.

3   See http://ivfnigerianewsupdates.blogspot.com

4   In Nigeria, stories of women delivering twins and triplets after many years of barrenness are popular and are commonly attributed to divine intervention. These stories are usually told on national television.

5   *Eshugbaye Eleko v. Government of Nigeria (1931)* AC 262 at 273 (1989) 1 N.W.L.R. (Part 97) 254.

6   I am quite aware of the initial controversies that surrounded the Report of the Committee of Inquiry into Human Fertilisation and Embryology, otherwise known as the Warnock Report, and the opposition of some religious groups to all forms of assisted reproduction.

7   See http://ivfnigerianewsupdates.blogspot.com Nigeria: 'Making Women Pregnant Gives Me Pleasure'. Wednesday, February 15, 2012.

8   See www.ivfbabiesnigeria.blogspot.com.ng '"How IVF saved us from childlessness" – Women count their blessings, become advocates'. Monday, December 21, 2015.

6

Beyond 'epistemicide': (Re)claiming humanity for Africa

In this book I have argued for a particular mode of engaging with endogenous practices, which takes into consideration unequal colonial encounters and the implications for social production and reproduction of cultural identities. This approach does not stand as an arbitrary romanticisation of a past that is almost obliterated from everyday consciousness in the postcolony. Rather, it has to do with reclaiming authenticity for African values outside of colonial epistemological benchmarks. It entailed questioning the most common assumptions on cultural unusualness. Indeed, the approach is about seeing Africa through Africa. In the identity of posthumous offspring in Ilupeju-Ekiti, I found a compelling story of inversion, conversion and, perhaps, resilience of Yoruba endogenous epistemology. Furthermore, I examined the challenges entails in endogenous kinship practices surviving in an environment dominated by Western constructs of family, parenthood and identity. I also explored the dilemma of the African mind in rationalising indigenous cultural practices and the epistemological debates provoked by cultural resilience. In all of this, I built on anthropological literature on family, kinship and identity in the Yoruba society. I also drew parallels between endogenous posthumous procreation and the contemporary practise of assisted reproduction technology as a way of deconstructing the idea of repugnancy woven around popular endogenous practices of Africans in the colonial and post-colonial era.

African epistemicide has since continued even after the vast colonial empires have long collapsed to give way for independent entities. The perpetrators are no longer the colonial authorities or the European Christian missionaries. Denigration of endogenous epistemology is a project continued by 'civilised Africans'. As I rounded off my fieldwork in Ilupeju-Ekiti, one particular comment that continually re-echoed in my mind was the claim that posthumous paternity belonged to the era when 'eyes were not yet opened'. Many of my informants expressed this sentiment and indeed believed that 'eyes are now opened', hence the disappearance of endogenous creative kinship practices. Although I had reservations about the terminology, especially when it is applied to endogenous values and cultural practices, I never for once contested the term *olaju* with my informants, which is widely applied among the Yoruba to operationalise the twin concepts of modernity and civilisation. But when one of them decided to show his mastery of the English language by describing posthumous paternity as barbaric, I felt I should engage with him constructively, and possibly offer him a free lesson in cultural relativism – one of anthropology's most cherished concepts. My informant, Pa Michael, now turned my student, was a man in his early 70s by my own estimation, and had been educated up to Teacher Training College level. He had been a primary school teacher in the community until some years ago when he retired from government service.

Pa Michael spoke of how Christianity has successfully transformed many of the cultural practices which he believed were inimical to the wellbeing of Africans in the pre-colonial era. Even when I tried to explain cultures as products of unique historical experiences of a people, his estimation of the Christian faith was total and characterised by idioms of redemption and salvation. The notion that he had of his community was a modern society where posthumous paternity, the subject in contention, no longer exists. Interestingly, he underscored the dynamic nature of culture when he suggested that 'cultural practices do have expiry dates', after which they become irrelevant even to their most immediate environments. In actual fact, only very few people including Pa Michael deny posthumous paternity as a cultural experience in the community. The contention, however, is that being a posthumous offspring in the contemporary society amounts to carrying an unusual identity.

What most often crossed my mind while writing this book is the institutionalisation of ignorance and arrogance on the matter of popular endogenous epistemologies. What really makes posthumous paternity repugnant to natural justice, or to equity and good conscience? What do these vague phrases actually mean? This kind of depiction was rebuffed by a set of first-generation African writers. But somehow, across the continent, people have managed to accept evaluation of their cultures on the basis of some peculiar foreign parameters. A colleague of mine, who incidentally is from the West, told me how he found the idea of cultural relativism objectionable. He was just uncomfortable with the way relativism restricts intervention in the case of unacceptable cultural occurrences that a sense of a universal ideal could have arrested. Although we were able to agree on some cultural universals, we tended to disagree on valuations in those instances when reality is detached from empiricism and meaning constantly derived from the invisible, the emotional, and the inexplicable (Nyamnjoh 2012). For Africans, generally, it may be that there is no longer a choice to be made regarding their epistemological preference. It may be that the past is gone beyond retrieval, but there is one notion Africans can yet correct: the past had authenticity within its very own milieu.

While views about posthumous offspring expressed by informants in this book may represent the prevailing attitude to an aspect of their endogenous epistemologies, it may be wrong to assume a total divorce of the people from the entire cultural system. In the case studies I examined, there are evidences of continued commitment to the traditional kinship ties although tensions have become noticeable. In all of this, the role of capital is pronounced. A process of illegitimating posthumous offspring cannot be wholly explained in terms of epistemological conversions of colonialism. Rather, it has to do with a new forms of economic competition introduced by colonialism. In essence, while Africans were initially made to see faults and flaws in their modes of thought and being, they have become more critical of these as new economic formations tend to appeal increasingly to their individual agency rather than to the more traditional collectivism of the past.

Scholars interested in the discourse of cultural change and resilience in Africa will probably find a few elements of Ilupeju posthumous paternity intriguing. First is the isolation from the mainstream Yoruba cultural repertoire. In this regard, I am tempted to see a resilience achieved far away from a mainstream as associated with the frontier nature of the community. But Tsing (2005) suggests frontiers as notoriously unstable, and one would ordinarily expect instability to manifest in rapid cultural change. Hence, there is an ambivalence of explanation as to where and when change and resilience may be achieved. While the frontier connection is strengthened by evidences of similar practices across the immediate ethno-regional border, care must also be taken not to depict the practice as a case of borrowing. Then, there is the secrecy that is built around a resilient cultural practice. Unlike in common examples of resilient practices being valorised and employed for constructing group identity, the reality of posthumous offspring is in most instances denied. It is then obvious that one is witnessing a practice which is perhaps in final stage of transition to obliteration. Of course, my effort in this book is not geared toward arresting the trend, as not only would that be overly ambitious, but useless too, considering the scale at which colonial epistemology has assumed the popular mode of thought. The idea that Africans are not proud of their past and have been wired to abhor it constitutes a dominant argument in this book.

Why has a process of conversion invariably assumed a point of no return? There is the obvious fact that many Africans lack deeper understanding of endogenous epistemologies. In the Yoruba world, and I believe the same applies to many cultures across Africa, being and belonging are not explained only in terms of physicality or biological connectedness. The kinship system presupposes a complex web of intersections and interactions between the worlds of the living and the dead. That this mode of thought is at variance with colonial epistemology does not necessarily invalidate it. I agree with Francis Nyamnjoh when he suggests that

> … such epistemologies are mainly dormant or invisible in scholarly circles because they are often ignored, caricatured or misrepresented in the categories of 'magic', 'witchcraft', 'sorcery', 'superstition', 'primitivism', 'savagery' and 'animism' inspired by the origins and dominance of Eurocentric social sciences. (2015, 3)

Unfortunately, Africans, especially the elites, are active participants in many policy contraptions that are meant to facilitate a complete obliteration of the African past. Recently, the government of Nigeria reportedly stopped the teaching of history as a subject in secondary schools; I learned such a policy also exists in other African countries. Meanwhile, in the teaching of religion, emphasis is on either Christian Religious Knowledge or Islamic Religious Knowledge. This kind of official disposition to the past raises difficult questions about African humanity, which a number of African scholars and Africanists have laboured to defend.

I have argued in this book that Western modernity also has as much explanation to make for their practices that in all respects share epistemological semblances with a quantum of pre-colonial African values that have been adjudged barbaric and reprehensible. It matters little whether such practices wear the garb of science or technology. I have called attention to practices of assisted reproduction, which are at variance with most known values about human procreation. This technology of being can also be repugnant to the African notion of 'natural justice, equity, and good conscience,' using the same language applied by colonial epistemology. The adoption, on a global scale, of practices that tend toward human commodification speaks to the unequal power relations that exist between the colonisers and the colonised, and the unchallenged right of a particular epistemology to solely produce 'obscenity' for the consumption of the rest of the world.

I met very few posthumous offspring during my research. For obvious reasons, their identity is private. Going underground has become a major strategy of resilience for many endogenous cultural practices, though concealment seems to be a phase in their transition to extinction. And even when posthumous offsprings' sense of self is marked by momentariness, and mostly self-contemplation, there is a way they constitute an unavoidable reality, which, though often denied, has lingered on. How long this will continue is however unknown. This situation is in itself akin to what obtains with other domains of endogenous culture where Africans feel shame about expressing their Africanness. For instance, many African elites no longer speak their mother tongues at home because they do not want their children to have 'accents'. This connects to the questions of self-belief and of the relationship between local knowledge and development often asked of post-colonial Africa. That these questions continue to be relevant shows the relentless nature of endogenous epistemologies, which continually unfold when complete disappearance is in contemplation, at least to illustrate the necessary but missing ideological basis of national development. The relegation of these values to furtively expressed aspects of the African life, no doubt, unleashes a sense of inferiority and subjugation in the continent's people rather than the pride and freedom that supposedly accompany independence.

Another way of looking at the passive resilience, which the practice of posthumous paternity definitely constitutes, is to think of the structures that colonial rule left behind to enforce subjectivity and compliance to its very own epistemology. First, the repugnancy doctrine has remained an active component of the legal system in Nigeria even though it has not been invoked as often since independence. The reason for its continued enforcement has more to do with an amenableness to Western ideals than of lack of judicial will. Second, the Christian religion forms an important sphere of an epistemological rebirth. Both the legalistic and religious assemblages are framed in terms of morality and acceptable behaviours. But the more important consideration with them is the way they intercept with the ideas of capitalist production and redistribution. The notion of a legitimacy as a social capital just makes compliance a necessary factor for participation in the social and economic sphere. It is in this regard that the contestations of the identity of posthumous offspring, which I discussed in Chapter 3, were made.

This book will have amounted to an academic whine if all that it does is offer an outline of problems. In other words, is there anything to be learned from interrogating a resilient popular endogenous practice? Can reflections on Africa's unequal colonial encounter serve as a point of engaging with issues of national development? What lessons can African intellectuals take from this as they struggle with the task of representing the actual problems of the continent?

There should be no mistake about the arguments being made here. These are not particularly geared toward suggesting a return to the past or a clampdown on Western lifestyles and mode of thoughts. The changes brought about by colonial epistemology are by no means reversible. However, it is not too much to demand from Africans, especially the elite class, a change of attitude toward the past, if for no other reason than to re-claim humanity for the continent. This goal may seem trivial, but it has value in terms of being a starting point for deconstructing colonial logics of a superior and more humanised worldview. It is within this ambit that the discussion in Chapter 5 perhaps finds relevance. There are other prospects we can identify with an agenda of humanising Africa, even when these appear far-fetched.

First, one can contemplate the level of creativity that may be enabled from perceiving the world in terms of interconnections and interdependences. But then, the image of boundlessness as illusion and superstition seems to be permanently etched in many minds in such a way that endogenous values are only constructed in relation to limitations rather than within the range of possibilities and alternatives they offer. Maybe purging people of the kind of bias of misrepresentation is a first step here. Much as Africans view sciences as key to the development of the continent, it appears they see science as what the West has achieved, or what they are currently doing, rather than a vision that transcends the realm of observable reality.

Now I must return to the conceptual and methodological issues addressed in this book. The literature on the second marriage option for the Yoruba widow has never been explicit in terms of what colonial anthropology described as the levirate system, particularly with respect to the position of posthumous offspring. However, in this book I have endeavoured to situate the rationale of posthumous paternity as a Yoruba kinship practice well beyond the idea of perpetuating the lineage of a deceased man. Although this aspect cannot be ignored, the practice as I have shown it is embedded in a particular cosmological orientation that sees life continuing in death, and the dead engaged in a back and forth movement between two worlds. I have deliberately avoided calling the system 'levirate' throughout this book because the practices I have described contain other variations that are not captured or envisaged by the levirate concept.

Two bodies of data are utilised in this book. The first emanates from fieldwork conducted in Ilupeju-Ekiti, and the second is derived from interviews and a series of discussions held with informants and colleagues within and outside the field context, basically on the subject of assisted reproductive technologies. The usefulness of the two sources is not only found in their producing the data the book needed to make its arguments. Their value is more or less contained in seeing meaning about an 'unusual' practice being connected to other contexts. It is a short story we have, for reasons that have been stated at different times in this book, but the implications are limitless, obviously extending beyond change and continuity of a cultural practice.

While a few scholarly works have associated the Yoruba with both widow inheritance and levirate marriage, others suggest widow inheritance as the only practice known to the people. Any of the perspectives could be seen as formulated on the notion of the Yoruba as culturally homogeneous. But in actual fact, what is valid may depend on which of the numerous Yoruba subgroups is in focus. More importantly, I have suggested in this book that widow inheritance likely occurs as another stage in the evolution of the levirate system.

Bibliography

Abimbola, K. 2006. *Yoruba Culture: A Philosophical Account*. London: Iroko Academy Publishers.

Abrahams, R. 1973. "Some Aspects of Levirate." In *The Character of Kinship*, edited by Jack Goddy, 163–174. Cambridge: Cambridge University Press.

Achebe, C. 1958. *Things Fall Apart*. London: Heinemann.

Achebe, C. 1961. *No Longer at Ease*. London: Heinemann.

Achebe, C. 1964. *Arrow of God*. London: Heinemann.

Ademiluka, S. 2003. "The impact of Christian missionary activity on the socio-cultural heritage of the O-kun Yoruba." In *Northeast Yorubaland: Studies in the history and culture of a frontier zone*, edited by A. Olukoju, Z. Apata, and O. Akinwunmi, 134–142. Ibadan, Nigeria: Rex Charles.

Akínnásò, F. 1980. "The Sociolinguistic Basis of Yorùbá Personal Names." *Anthropological Linguistics* 22 (7): 275–304.

Akintoye, S. 1969. "The North-Eastern Yoruba Districts and the Benin Kingdom." *Journal of the Historical Society of Nigeria* IV (4): 539–553.

Akintoye, S. 1971. *Revolution and Power Politics in Yorubaland, 1840-1893: Ibadan Expansion and the Rise of Ekitiparapo*. London: Longman Group.

Amanze, J. 1998. *African Christianity in Botswana*. Gweru, Zimbabwe: Mambo Press.

Amin, S. 1972. "Underdevelopment and Dependence in Black Africa – Origins and Contemporary Forms." *Journal of Modern African Studies* 10 (4): 503–24. doi:10.1017/S0022278X00022801.

Appadurai, A. 1996. *Modernity at Large: Cultural Dimensions of Globalisation*. Minneapolis: University of Minnesota Press.

Asiedu-Akrofi, D. 1989. "Judicial Recognition and Adoption of Customary Law in Nigeria." *American Journal of Comparative Law* 37 (3): 571–93. doi:10.2307/840092.

Awolalu, J., and P. Dopamu. 2005. *West African Traditional Religion*. Ibadan: Macmillan Nigeria Publishers Limited.

Bascom, W. 1969. *The Yoruba of Southwestern Nigeria*. New York: Holt, Rinehart, and Winston.

Bloch, M. 1988. "Death and the concept of person." In *On the Meaning of Death: Essays on Mortuary Rituals and Eschatological Beliefs*, edited by S. Cederroth, C. Corlin, and J. Lindstrom, 11–29. Uppsala: Acta Universitatis Uppsaliensis.

Bourdieu, P. 1984. *Distinction: A Social Critique of the Judgment of Taste*. London: Routledge.

Cannell, F. 1990. "Concepts of parenthood: The Warnock Report, the Gillick Debate, and Modern Myths." *American Ethnologist* 17 (4): 667–86. doi:10.1525/ae.1990.17.4.02a00040.

Cohen, A. 1994. *Self Consciousness: An Alternative Anthropology of Identity*. London: Routledge.

Coker, G. B. A. 1966. *Family Property among the Yorubas*. London: Sweet and Maxwell. doi:10.4324/9780203418987.

Cooper, F. 2005. *Colonialism in Question: Theory, Knowledge, History*. University of California Press.

Davies, D. 2000. "Robert Hertz: The Social Triumph Over Death." *Mortality* 5 (1): 97–102. doi:10.1080/713685991.

Eades, J. 1980. *The Yoruba Today*. Cambridge: Cambridge University Press.

Ebeku, K. 1994. "The Legal Status of Nigerian Children Born by a Widow: Chinweze v. Masi Revisited." *Journal of African Law* 38 (1): 46–60. doi:10.1017/S0021855300011451.

Eriksen, T. 2010. *Ethnicity and Nationalism: Anthropological Perspectives*. 3rd ed. London, New York: Pluto Press.

Evans-Pritchard, E. E. 1945. *Some Aspects of Marriage and the Family among the Nuer*. Rhodes-Livingstone Papers.

Evans-Pritchard, E. E. 1951. *Kinship and Marriage among the Nuer*. Oxford: Claredon Press.

Fanon, F. 1967. *The Wretched of the Earth*. Harmondsworth: Penguin.

Filipović, M. 1958. "Vicarious Paternity among Serbs and Croats." *Southwestern Journal of Anthropology* 14 (2): 156–67. doi:10.1086/soutjanth.14.2.3628955.

Forde, D. 1951. *The Yoruba-Speaking Peoples of South-Western Nigeria: Ethnographic Survey of Africa, Part IV*. London: International African Institute.

Foucault, M. 1997. "What is Enlightenment." In *The essential works of Michel Foucault 1954-1984*, edited by P. Rabinow and J. Faubion, 303–320. New York: New Press.

Foucault, M. 1988. "Technologies of the Self." In T*echnologies of the Self: A Seminar with Michel Foucault*, edited by L. H. Martin, H. Gutman and P. H. Hutton, 16-49. Amherst: University of Massachusetts Press.

Geertz, C. 1973. *The Interpretation of Cultures*. Basic Books.

Geertz, C. 1983. *Local Knowledge: Further Essays in Interpretive Anthropology*. Basic Books.

Gluckman, M. 1950. "Kinship and marriage among the Lozi of Northern Rhodesia and the Zulu of Natal." In *African Systems of Kinship and Marriage*, edited by D. Forde and A. R. Radcliffe-Brown, 166–206. London: Oxford University Press.

Goffman, E. 1969. *The Presentation of Self in Everyday Life*. London: Penguin.

Gray, R. 1964. "Introduction." In *The Family Estate in Africa*, edited by R. F. Gray and P. H. Gulliver, 1–34. London: Routledge and Kegan Paul Ltd.

Grillo, R. 1999. "An African Railwayman is a Railwayman' ... Or the subject of the Subject of the Subject." In *Identity and Affect: Experiences of Identity in a Globalising World*, edited by J. R. Campbell and A. Rew, 227–250. London, Sterling and Virginia: Pluto Press.

Hartley, S. 1975. *Illegitimacy*. Oakland: University of California Press.

Hertz, R. 1960 [1907]. "A Contribution to the Study of the Collective Representation of Death." In *Death and the Right Hand*, edited by R. Hertz, Trans. R. and C. Needham, 25–28. London: Cohen and West. [Contribution à une étude sur la représentation collective de la mort. Année]

Sociologique 10 (1905–6): 48–137.

Kirwen, M. 1979. *African Widows*. New York: Orbis Books.

Kopytoff, I. 1987. The African Frontier: The Reproduction of Traditional African Societies. Bloomington and Indianapolis: Indiana University Press.

Korieh, C. J. 1996. Widowhood among the Igbo of Eastern Nigeria. Thesis submitted for the Degree of Master of Philosophy in History, University of Bergen, Norway, Bergen Spring.http://www.ub.uib.no/elpub/1996/h/506001/korieh/chima.html

Laing, J. 2006. "Artificial Reproduction, Blood Relatedness, and Human

Identity." *Monist* 89 (4): 548–66. doi:10.5840/monist20068947.

Law, R. 1991. *The Oyo Empire, C. 1600-C. 1836: A West African Imperialism in the Era of the Atlantic Slave Trade*. Oxford University Press.

Lawuyi, B. 2015. *Nigeria as a Market Metaphor: The Scenario of Visibility, Representation and Power in the Public Space*. Ibadan, Nigeria: Ibadan University Press.

Lloyd, P. 1955. "The Yoruba Lineage." *Africa* 25 (3): 235–51. doi:10.2307/1157104.

Lu, S., and G. Fine. 1995. "The Presentation of Ethnic Authenticity: Chinese Food in Social Accomplishment." *Sociological Quarterly* 36 (3): 535–53. doi:10.1111/j.1533-8525.1995.tb00452.x.

MacGaffey, W. 1981. "African Ideology and Belief: A Survey." *African Studies Review* 24 (2-3): 227–274. doi:10.2307/523905.

Mignolo, W. 2011. T*he Darker Side of Western Modernity: Global Futures, Decolonial Options*. Durham: Duke University Press.

Malinowski, B. 1929. "Practical Anthropology." *Africa* 2 (1): 22–38. doi:10.2307/1155162

Mbiti, J. 1969. *African Religions and Philosophy*. London: Heinemann Press.

Morton-Williams, P. 1960. "Yoruba responses to the fear of death." *Africa* 30 (1): 34–40. doi:10.2307/1157739.

Mosse, D. 1999. "Responding to Subordination: Identity and Change among South Indian Untouchable Castes." In *Identity and Affect: Experiences of Identity in a Globalising World*, edited by J. R. Campbell and A. Rew, 64–104. London, Sterling and Virginia: Pluto Press.

Mudimbe, V. 1988. *The Invention of Africa: Gnosis, Philosophy, and the Order of Knowledge*. Bloomington, Indianapolis: Indiana University Press.

Mugambi, J. 2002. *Christianity and African Culture*. Nairobi: Action Publishers.

Nyamnjoh, F. 2004. "From Publish or Perish to Publish and Perish: What 'Africa's 100 Best Books' Tell Us About Publishing Africa." *Journal of Asian and African Studies* 39 (5): 331–55. doi:10.1177/0021909604051185.

Nyamnjoh, F. 2012. "'Potted Plants in Greenhouses': A Critical Reflection on the Resilience of Colonial Education in Africa." *Journal of Asian and African Studies* 47 (2): 129–54. doi:10.1177/0021909611417240.

Nyamnjoh, F. 2015. "Amos Tutuola and the Elusiveness of Completeness." *Stichproben. Wiener Zeitschrift für kritische Afrikastudien* 15: 1–47.

Oboler, R. 1986. "Nandi Widows." In *Widows in African Societies*, edited by B. Potash, 66–83. Stanford, California: Stanford University Press.

Ogbu, J. 1978. "African Bridewealth and Women's Status." *American Ethnologist* 5 (2): 241–62. doi:10.1525/ae.1978.5.2.02a00040.

Okolo, C. 1992. "Self as a Problem in African Philosophy." *International Philosophical Quarterly* XXXII (4): 477–485.

Okonjo, K. 1992. "Aspects of Continuity and Change in Mate-Selection Among the Igbo West of the River Niger." *Journal of Comparative Family Studies* 23 (3): 330–60.

Okri, B. 1991. *The Famished Road*. London: Vintage.

Olanisebe, S., and O. Oladosu. 2014. "Levirate marriage amongst the Hebrews and widow's inheritance amongst the Yoruba: A comparative investigation." *Verbum et Ecclesia* 35 (1): 1–7. doi:10.4102/ve.v35i1.826.

Ololajulo, B. 2016. "'Eating with one spoon': Zoning, power rotation and political corruption in Nigeria." *African Studies* 75 (1): 153-169.

Oni, B. 1991. "Contemporary Courtship and Marriage Practices among the Yoruba." *International Journal of Sociology of the Family* 21 (2): 145–60.

Oyono, F. 1956. *Le Vieux Nègre et La Médaille*. Paris: Rene Julliard.

Oyono, F. 1960. *Chemin d'Europe*. Paris: Rene Julliard.

p'Bitek, O. (Original work published 1967) 1984. *Song of Lawino; Song of Ocol*. Oxford: Heinemann.

p'Bitek, O. (Original work published 1966) 1989. *Song of Lawino*. Nairobi: East African Educational Publishers.

Palgi, P., and H. Abramovitch. 1984. "Death: Across-cultural perspective." *Annual Review of Anthropology* 13 (1): 385–417. doi:10.1146/annurev.an.13.100184.002125.

Peterson, R. 2005. "In Search of Authenticity." *Journal of Management Studies* 42 (5): 1083–98. doi:10.1111/j.1467-6486.2005.00533.x.

Potash, B. 1986. "Wives of the Grave: Widows in a Rural Luo Community." In *Widows in African Societies*, edited by B. Potash, 44–65. Stanford, California: Stanford University Press.

Poulter, S. 1977. "Marriage, Divorce and Legitimacy in Lesotho." *Journal of African Law* 21 (1): 66–78. doi:10.1017/S002185530000855X.

Radcliffe-Brown, A. 1950. "Introduction." In *African Systems of Kinship and Marriage*, edited by D. Forde and A. R. Radcliffe-Brown, 1–85. London: Oxford University Press.

Rew, A., and J. Campbell. 1999. "The Political Economy of Identity and Affect." In *Identity and Affect: Experiences of Identity in a Globalising World*, edited by J. Campbell and A. Rew, 1–38. London, Sterling and Virginia: Pluto Press.

Rivière, P. 1985. "Unscrambling Parenthood: The Warnock Report." *Anthropology Today* 1 (4): 2–7. doi:10.2307/3032682.

Rodney, W. 1972. *How Europe Underdeveloped Africa*. Nairobi, Kampala, Dar es Salaam: East African Educational Publishers.

Rowland, R. 1985. "The Social and Psychological Consequences of Secrecy in A.I.D. Programmes." *Social Science and Medicine* 21:391-396.

Schapera, I. 1950. "Kinship and marriage among the Tswana." In *African Systems of Kinship and Marriage*, edited by D. Forde and A. R. Radcliffe-Brown, 140–165. London: Oxford University Press.

Shizha, E., and M. Kariwo, eds. 2011. *Education and Development in Zimbabwe: A Social, Political and Economic Analysis*. Rotterdam: Sense Publishers. doi:10.1007/978-94-6091-606-9.

Schwab, W. B. 1958. "The Terminology of Kinship and Marriage among the Yoruba." *Africa* 28 (4): 301–13. doi:10.2307/1157637.

Shapiro, W. 2009. *Partible Paternity and Anthropological Theory: The Construction of an Ethnographic Fantasy*. Lanham, Maryland: University Press of America.

Shore, C., R. G. Abrahams, Jane F. Collier, Carol Delaney, Robin Fox, Ronald Frankenberg, Helen S. Lambert, et al. 1992. "Virgin Births and Sterile Debates: Anthropology and the New Reproductive Technologies." *Current Anthropology* 33 (3): 295–314. doi:10.1086/204071.

Simpson, B. 2001. "Making 'Bad' Deaths 'Good': The Kinship Consequences of Posthumous Conception." *Journal of the Royal Anthropological Institute* 7 (1): 1–18. doi:10.1111/1467-9655.00047.

Simpson, B. 2013. "Managing Potential in Assisted Reproductive Technologies: Reflections on Gifts, Kinship, and the Process of Vernacularisation." *Current Anthropology* 54 (S7): S87–96. doi:10.1086/670173.

Sökefeld, M. 1999. "Debating Self, Identity, and Culture in Anthropology." *Current Anthropology* 40 (4): 417–48.

Soyinka, W. 1975. *Death and the king's horseman*. Eyre Methuen.

Taye, O. 2013. "Questionable but Unquestioned Beliefs: A Call for a Critical Examination of Yoruba Culture." *Thought and Practice: A Journal of the Philosophical Association of Kenya* (PAK) 5 (2): 81–101.

Tsing, A. 2005. *Friction: An Ethnography of Global Connection*. Princeton University Press.

Turner, V. 1969. *The Ritual Process: Structure and Antistructure*. Chicago: Aldine Publishing Corporation.

Tutuola, A. 1952. *The Palm-Wine Drinkard*. London: Faber and Faber.

Wagner, S. 2013. "The making and unmaking of an unknown soldier." *Social Studies of Science* 43 (5): 631–656. doi:10.1177/0306312713484646.

Warnier, J. 1993. "The King as a Container in the Cameroon Grassfields." *Paideuma* 39: 303–19.

Warnier, J. 2007. *The Pot-King: The Body and Technologies of Power*. Leiden: Brill. doi:10.1163/ej.9789004152175.i-325.

Weisberg, D. 2009. *Levirate Marriage and the Family in Ancient Judaism*. Lebanon: Brandeis University Press. doi:10.26812/9781584657811.

Index

A

abiku (spirit-children) 10
academic publishing 14
Achebe, Chinua 9–10, 12–14
Africanness and Western modernity, contradictions 3
ancestors, interconnections in Yoruba epistemologies 8–10, 11–12
anthropological treatment of self and identity 7
assisted reproduction
    anonymity 82
    and the cultural construction of adultery 92–94
    language of 81–82
    name-calling 83
    paternity 82–83
    rightness and wrongness 4–5
    unnatural, feelings towards 82
    Warnock Report 83
    see also in vitro fertilisation

B

Baba Ojo's story 40–41
bewitchment 45
born from another man's hands *see* posthumous offspring

C

Chinweze v. Masi dispute 84–85
Christianity
    colonialism 12–13
    and informants' attitude to practice of posthumous paternity 50–51
    Methodist church position on posthumous paternity 59–61
colonialism
    academic publishing 14
    Christianity 12–13
    education system 14
    epistemicide 14–15
    institutionalised government 13–14
    repugnancy principle 14, 22
    vernacular languages, prohibition 14

Index

container kings 11
cultural authenticity *see* Yoruba cultural authenticity and posthumous paternity
cultural obscenity view 66, 86–87
cultural resilience 3–4, 7

D

Diop, Birago 9
disaggregated paternity 88–89
doctor as helper 89–91
dual kinship identities 36–37

E

endogenous epistemologies 7, 12, 18, 25–26, 31, 44, 61, 67–68, 75, 85–86, 96–98, 100
epistemicide 2
    colonial 14–15
    postcolonial 96–97
Eshugbaye Eleko v. Government of Nigeria (1931) case 85

F

family and identity 42–43
forces of political economy as drivers of change 72
Fowobi 79, 81–82

I

identity 18–20
    concept in social anthropology 18–19
    and family 42–43
    gender dynamics 35
    of posthumous offspring 19
    state of incompleteness 20
    technologies of the self 19
identity locale, relevance 54
identity of posthumous offspring
    secrecy 26–28
    threats to reveal 46
identity power 56
Ile-Ife migration narrative 65
informants' attitude to practice of posthumous paternity 50–51
inheritance, levitate vs widow inheritance 17
institutionalised government 13–14
in vitro fertilisation 86–88
    doctor as 'helper' 89–90, 90–91
    incest risk 92

language of help 90
paternity as cultural construction 91–92
secrecy 94
sperm donor as 'helper' 91
Warnock Report 92
see also assisted reproduction

L
land as an economic good 48
language of assisted reproduction 81–82
language of help 90
legal status of children born by widows in Nigeria 84–85
legitimacy
    borders of 48–53
    concept of legitimacy 49
    definition of legitimate children 49–50
    hierarchy of kinship, implied 52
    land as an economic good 48
    limits of economic rights 51–52
    political economics of lineage identity 50
    rights to family patrimony, contests over 52
legitimacy and the identity of power
    bribery 56–57
    identity and political exclusion 57–58
    identity locale, relevance of 54
    identity power 56
    participation in economic processes 58–59
    patrilineal vs matrilineal lineage 56–57
    political marginalisation and privilege 54
    political power as a resource 53–54
    struggle for power as lacking in moral basis 58
    Taiwo's story 54–55
    zoning of small offices to wards and identity groups 55–56
    see also church position on posthumous paternity
levirate and widow inheritance 15–18, 69–72, 101
    as alien trait 71
    duality of widow remarriage options 71–72
    forces of political economy as drivers of change 72
    as Ilupeju import 71
    inheritance 17
    succession rights 17
    widow inheritance as a successor of levirate 69–72
liminal space, Interconnections in Yoruba epistemologies 10–12
lineage perpetuation, necessity of 6

Index

M
matrilineal vs patrilineal lineage 56–57
Methodist church position on posthumous paternity 59–61
multiple births 86–87

N
name-calling of children born through assisted reproduction 83
necessity for lineage perpetuation 6

O
Okri, Ben 10
Okuwobi, Very Rev, on posthumous paternity 59–61
Omoluabi philosophy 65
Onan, biblical story about posthumous paternity 60–61

P
paternity
    assisted reproduction 82–83
    as cultural construction 91–92
patrilineal vs matrilineal lineage 56–57
p'Bitek, Okot 12, 14
piggy-banks 11
political exclusion 39, 52
political marginalisation and privilege 54
political power as a resource 53–54
posthumous offspring
    as 'born from another man's hands' 28–31
    genitor, status of 29–30
    Ilupeju paternity ideology 29
    legitimacy of children 30–31
    political exclusion 31–34
    see also identity of posthumous offspring
posthumous paternity documented in other African countries 5
power 4–5, 46–47, 53–55, 58

Q
quarrels between wives 45–46

R
reclaiming humanity for Africa 96–101
    ancestors 101
    cultural relativism 97
    frontiers 98

Index

　　　language 99
　　　passive resilience 100
　　　secrecy 98, 99
　　　technology assisted reproduction 99
recognition of biological father 37–38
repugnancy doctrine 47, 84–89, 100
　　　Chinweze v. Masi dispute 84–85
　　　Eshugbaye Eleko v. Government of Nigeria (1931) case 85
　　　legal status of children born by widows in Nigeria 84–85
　　　multiple births 86–87
　　　social stigma associated with IVF 88
　　　and traditional cultural practices 86
　　　In vitro fertilisation 86–88
　　　Warnock Committee 76, 79, 83, 88–89

S

secrecy around in vitro fertilisation 94
secrecy of identity of posthumous offspring 26–28, 67–68
　　　benefits and disadvantages 27–28
　　　informants' attitude to practice 28, 35
self and identity 41–43
　　　anthropological treatment 7
self presentation vignettes
　　　Baba Ojo's story 40–41
　　　Bayo's story 37–40
　　　family and identity 42–43
　　　family tension risk for genitor 41
　　　genitor's relationship with children 40–41
　　　individual differences in confronting identity 42
　　　omo oku orun (orphan) self-description 34
　　　political exclusion 31–34, 39
　　　recognition of biological father 37–38
　　　relationship with genitor's offspring and lineage 39
　　　self and identity 41–43
　　　Taiwo's story 31–34
　　　Tayo's story 34–37
　　　wedding eve 36
　　　widow inheritor selection 40
self-subordination 51
small offices, zoning to wards and identity groups 55–56
social stigma associated with IVF 88
socio-economy of bridewealth 6
Soyinka, Wole 10, 14
spaces of cultural authenticity 65

Index

sperm donor as 'helper' 91
spirit-children *(abiku)* 10
state of incompleteness 20
subordinate social identities 51
succession rights, levirate vs widow inheritance 17

T

Taiwo's story
    legitimacy and the identity of power 54–55
    rank in lineage 52
    self presentation vignettes 31–34
Tayo's story 34–37
technologies of the self 19
technology mediated adultery 92–93
Tutuola, Amos 6, 10–11, 23

U

Ubuntu 6
unburied dead, spirits of 10

V

vernacular languages, prohibition 14

W

Warnock Report 83, 88–89, 92
Western assimilation 2
Western modernity 3, 12–14, 19, 21, 25–27, 40, 76, 99
widow inheritance 15–18, 21, 38, 101
    as a successor of levirate 69–72
widow inheritor selection 40

Y

Yoruba cultural authenticity and posthumous paternity
    cultural obscenity view 66
    customs, lack of uniformity 65–66
    dialects 66
    ideal being 65
    Ile-Ife 65
    philosophy of *Omoluabi* 65
    political culture 65
    secrecy of identity of living posthumous offspring 67–68
    widows' remarriage practices 68–69

Yoruba epistemologies, interconnections 8–12
 ancestors 8–10, 11–12
 container kings 11
 piggy-banks 11
 spirit-children *(abiku)* 10
 unburied dead, spirits of 10

Z
zoning of small offices to wards and identity groups 55–56

www.ingramcontent.com/pod-product-compliance
Lightning Source LLC
Chambersburg PA
CBHW081827230426
43668CB00017B/2402